YOUTH VIOLENCE

How to Protect Your Kids

KEVIN GUEST

with Donald Cowper
and Andrew Haynes

A COMMUNITIES AGAINST YOUTH VIOLENCE BOOK

Youth Violence: How To Protect Your Kids

A Communities Against Youth Violence Book

Published in Canada by
Communities Against Youth Violence
621 Milverton Blvd., Toronto, Ontario, M4C 1X8, Canada

Guest, Kevin
Youth Violence: How To Protect Your Kids

ISBN 0-9681226-0-4
copyright © 1997 by Communities Against Youth Violence

Design by Late Harvest Entertainment Corp.

Printed and bound in Canada

About the Author

Kevin Guest is a police officer with the Metropolitan Toronto Police Service. He has spent several years on the Street Crime Unit dealing with young offenders and talking to students all across the city of Toronto. He has produced a documentary for the police service entitled *Tackle Violence* which has been seen by over 80,000 students in Toronto. He has appeared on *Global TV First National*, *TV Ontario*, and City TV's *Breakfast Television* talking about the problem of youth violence. He lives in Toronto with his wife Trish and their son Torin.

About CAYV

Communities Against Youth Violence is an organization dedicated to reducing youth violence. CAYV publishes books and runs seminars that teach parents how to protect their kids from youth violence.

To Torin

ACKNOWLEDGMENTS

A few years ago I had an idea to write a book about the problem of youth violence. It remained just an idea until I discussed it with my longtime friend Erik Tallmeister who suggested I stop thinking about it and do it. Erik got me in touch with two writers, Donald Cowper and Andy Haynes, who were equally excited about the project. After many long months, the project finally made its way out of my imagination and onto paper.

While working on this book I met hundreds of other people who care as strongly as I do about protecting our kids and trying to solve the problem of youth violence. Many of these people helped me get this book to print, and without their help this book simply would not exist. I am truly grateful.

Special thanks go to Dr. Fred Mathews, a community psychologist at Central Toronto Youth Services and a teacher in the graduate school of the University of Toronto. I have learned a lot about youth violence from talking to him and reading his research. He also encouraged me to write this book when it was still merely an idea in my head. I thank him for that and for the foreword he wrote.

I am indebted to John Muise, my colleague at the police service. He inspired me to keep plugging away at this book during its initial stages, and he was immensely helpful in bringing it to fruition. John Muise is also a member of Communities Against Youth Violence.

Many others at the police service helped make this book a reality. Among them are Staff Inspector Ron Taverner, Staff Inspector William Fordham, all the members of the 5 District Street Crime Unit, and Chief David Boothby.

Thanks go to Stu Auty, head of the Canadian Safe School Task Force, for his support, encouragement and thoughtful discussion.

I must also thank a large number of school principals and teachers. Among them are Fred James at Bathurst Heights; Bob Heath, Holly

Lipsett, Nadine Segal, and Brian Punchard of the Scarborough Board of Education; Rick Cunningham and Susan Hiraishi of the East York Board; Bryan McCormick of the Toronto Board; Leo Herskowitz, principal at Don Valley Jr. High; John Gibson, principal at Hodgson Sr. Public; Brian Currah, David Wells, and Erich Leherer at Malvern Collegiate Institute; Tony Tumenari and Rosemary Evans at Leaside High School.

For allowing me to speak to their students about youth violence, I'd like to thank the School Boards of Toronto, York, East York, North York, Etobicoke and Scarborough. Thanks also to the Metropolitan Toronto Separate School Board and to Upper Canada College.

For their support, I thank Jean Hewitt at the Ministry of Education of Ontario, Beverly Topping of Today's Parent Group, Tom Ambas, Willy and Patty Ewaschiuk, Kim Diamond at The Granite Club, Crime Stoppers Canada, and especially Adrian Harvey.

A number of people read various manuscripts and gave very valuable feedback. I'd like to thank Ann Margaret Oberst, Christine Rooney, Teri Cowper, Dara Cowper, Alan and Carmela Tallmeister, John Harding, and Kaili Sermat.

I thank Eric Conroy of Community Programs for his time and for opening doors for our organization.

Thanks goes to my copy editor, Colin Ground, for his expert editing and many insightful suggestions. However, I take full responsibility for any errors that still remain in the book.

Donald and Andy would like to pass along their heartfelt thanks to Ann Margaret and Christine for all of their encouragement, support and invaluable help throughout the entire project. They would also like to thank Leonid Rozenberg.

And last, I'd like to thank my parents, Roger and Patricia Guest, and my wife Trish for their patience and loving support.

Kevin Guest
November 11, 1996

TABLE OF CONTENTS

FOREWORD

I have spent my entire professional life as an educator, psychologist, and social scientist investigating controversial subject matter involving children and youth, particularly high-risk teens. After many years of studying youth gangs, school-based crime, and other forms of teen violence, I have found that parents and families have the strongest impact on the lives of children. In fact, firm, fair and involved parents are the least likely to see their children involved in serious anti-social, violent, or delinquent behaviour.

When Kevin first spoke to me about his idea for this book, I was encouraged. He wanted to speak directly to the people he thought could make the biggest difference – parents – using simple and easy-to-follow examples. I think he has succeeded.

Youth Violence: How To Protect Your Kids is insightful, original and filled with straightforward solutions parents can put into action right away. Kevin's personal style grounds the discussion in everyday life interactions and brings out the thoughts, feelings, and questions of concerned adults and youth in an accessible and direct manner. It gives us a frontline perspective on the problem of youth violence in the 1990s. *Youth Violence: How To Protect Your Kids* makes a valuable contribution to the work of keeping our schools and communities safe.

Fred Mathews, M.Ed., Ph.D., C.Psych.
Community Psychologist, Central Toronto Youth Services
Associate Instructor, Dept. of Applied Psychology, OISE/
University of Toronto

INTRODUCTION

Today a 15-year-old boy was stabbed to death on his way home from school. His two attackers were also high-school students. My own son Torin is only a year old now, but my wife Trish and I are gravely concerned about how dangerous our streets and schools will be by the time he turns 15. So, I feel we must find a solution to the frightening problem of youth violence before it's too late for all of our sons and daughters.

As a police officer I am directly involved with kids on a daily basis, dealing with young offenders and talking to students all across the city. I have seen bullying, extortion, vandalism and gangs blossom in our schools and communities – this trend cannot continue. That's why I wrote *Youth Violence: How To Protect Your Kids*. I hope it helps us all to reduce youth violence by encouraging more communication between parents, children, teachers and police. And I hope it helps you to protect your own children.

The book follows a series of parents meetings that take place throughout the school year, and each session is full of engaging stories and discussion. The parents group and the stories I tell are all based upon my real life experiences but, of course, all the names and settings have been changed to protect the people involved.

In this book, we will explore the dangers your children face, and learn how to protect them. I'm glad you're reading it, because it contains all of the information and the concrete solutions I wish I had the time to tell each parent individually.

PART 1

Your Child's World

1

THE FIRST PARENTS MEETING

As I pulled into the parking lot of my old school for the first parents meeting of the year, I realized how nervous I was about speaking. Each of these parents meetings is crucial because police and parents must successfully communicate in order to keep our kids safe. But sometimes opening up the dialogue is hard because parents are divided on the issue – some think their kids are safe, some are worried to death. Yet somehow we must come to an agreement about the size of the problem and how we can help. We need to find solutions quickly, because children are getting hurt everyday.

Through the windshield I saw three kids leaving the school. They must have been in grade eight, but they seemed so much bigger than the kids I went to school with. Certainly their clothes made them look bigger – baggy jeans, oversized parkas, and huge basketball shoes. To many adults, kids dressed like this look stupid, but sometimes these kids are sending a clear message – don't mess with me. They're too young to have large muscles, so they bulk up with clothing and feel bigger, tougher. It gives them attitude.

These kids are not only more aggressive than me and my friends ever were, they are also getting into more serious trouble than we did. When I was in grade eight, a couple of kids might have smoked and there was the occasional fight. I can only remember one instance when a police officer was called to the school, and that was for the theft of a student's knapsack from the lunch room. Now there is a more or less constant police presence in a lot of schools. When we're not responding to calls for criminal activity, we're giving lectures, talking to students, or creating partnerships with teachers and principals on the growing problem of violence and gangs in communities and schools.

I grabbed my briefcase and got out of the car, stepping into the cool evening. The arch that framed the front entrance to the school loomed in front of me and the light from the empty foyer shone through the glass doors. I'm not used to seeing schools so quiet.

Usually I am at schools during the day when the corridors are packed with noisy kids. As I walk by some of the kids bristle, others just ignore me, but some say hello. They're happy to see me, because they're the type of kids who like knowing a cop is around. Kids approach me all the time with complaints of bullying, harassment, and extortion. A lot of them tell me they know kids who carry weapons. It's sad that they're afraid in what should be a safe place to learn. Often they feel like they're on their own, many tell me they wish their parents really knew what was going on. I have met parents who are shocked to find out what pressures are placed on their children everyday in these halls.

I walked into the classroom that had been booked for our meeting and threw my briefcase on the teacher's desk. A dozen or so mothers and half-a-dozen fathers were sitting behind small desks around the room.

John Gillespie, the principal, walked up to the front and said, "Hello everyone. When we met last month we all voiced our concern over the increase in violence in our city's schools. I know the stabbing of the grade-nine student at the high school down the street really shocked us all. It was such an eye-opener because I'm sure none of us believed it could happen in our neighbourhood. If you remember at that meeting we took a look at the situation in our own school, and although we have had a few incidents, fortunately none were very serious. However, we all agreed that we shouldn't be complacent. Instead of waiting for something serious to happen here, we decided to do everything we can to ensure that our kids are safe, whether they're at school or playing in the neighbourhood. The last thing we want is one of our kids getting hurt. We decided the first step we should take is learning everything we can about youth violence – how big the problem really is, why it happens, and what we can do about it. So, we've invited P.C. Kevin Guest from the Community Relations

Department of the Metro Toronto Police Service to speak to us. Kevin has spent years dealing with youth crime, first as a cop on the streets, and then later developing programs and talking to kids in our schools. Kevin will be coming once a month to our regular Monday night meetings throughout the school year – until next March at least. He'll be talking about different aspects of the problem. Kevin. . . ."

"Thank you, John," I said as I stood up and straightened my jacket. "Good evening, everyone. This is a topic that is very important to me and, after tonight, I hope it is for you too. I have very real fears about my own son, because of what I read in the paper everyday and see while I'm doing my job. I don't want my son growing up in a violent society. I want him to be safe.

"As John said, youth violence is serious, very serious. We've all read or heard stories about kids committing violent crimes. In recent weeks we learned that an 11-year-old boy raped a 13-year-old girl, an armed pair of grade ten boys hijacked a school bus full of kids, an 18-year-old boy was clubbed to death with a baseball bat by a group of kids at a shopping mall, a 14-year-old boy was beaten to death by another 14-year-old, and a 17-year-old boy was stabbed in an after-school encounter at a local subway station.

"Kids kill and kids are dying, but there's actually much more to the problem of youth violence than that. Those crimes I mentioned are just the visible tip of the iceberg. In reality the majority of youth violence happens on a lower, more insidious level and involves harassment, threats and extortion as preludes to the act of violence. So we'll be focusing for the next seven months on the entire spectrum of youth violence, not just the big media cases. And we'll be learning how to protect our kids.

"Today I'll be introducing the three most important points to understand about youth violence. We all need to be familiar with them in order to tackle the problem successfully. But before we go into these three points, I would like to start by telling you about a case I worked on earlier this year. This story shows how violent behaviour evolves and how easily some children become victims.

JAMIE'S STORY

"Jamie was thirteen, just starting grade 8 at a school in a good neighbourhood. He played soccer and volleyball. He enjoyed science and math, and had a small group of friends. He knew who the bad kids were and he was smart enough to stay away from them.

"He thought that if he stayed away he'd be safe. But three weeks into the year, he found out he was wrong. One afternoon as he was walking across the school yard on his way home, he was confronted by a new kid named Rick. He wasn't any bigger or tougher than Jamie, but Rick had a group of friends to back him up. They spread out in a circle to surround Jamie, and blocked his way out of the school yard. Rick leaned into Jamie's face and blurted, 'Where do you think you're going.' Nervous, Jamie replied, 'I'm going home.' Still in his face, Rick said, 'Not until I let you. I got something to say. I heard the kids in the other grade eight class talking about you. They said they're gonna get ya, teach you a lesson.' Jamie said, 'Why? What did I do?' Rick said, 'I don't know. That's your problem. I just know they're gonna kill ya.'

"Rick, of course, had the solution to Jamie's problem. He told Jamie he needed a knife. Scared, Jamie told Rick he didn't have a knife. Rick couldn't believe that Jamie didn't already have one. The other kids kept telling Jamie over and over again that he was dead, scaring the crap out of him. Then Rick said, 'I'll sell you mine for twenty bucks.' When Jamie said he didn't want it, and that he wouldn't even know how to use it, Rick and his friends laughed. Rick pushed Jamie and said, 'Come on, man, only twenty bucks.'

"Cornered, confused, and completely intimidated, Jamie reluctantly agreed to buy the knife, but he didn't have the money. Rick accused him of lying and said he'd better bring the money tomorrow. He told Jamie that he wouldn't see the knife until he coughed up. And if he didn't buy the knife he'd be dead.

"That night Jamie felt completely alone. He spent the whole night in his room worrying, stressed out about what to do. He was scared to death of Rick, and terrified of the gang. He didn't know what he was going to do. He was afraid to tell his parents because he thought they wouldn't believe him and that even if they did and tried to intervene, Rick or the guys in his group would beat him up. He hoped the problem would just go away.

"But the next day, after school, they cornered him again. Choking back tears, he told them, 'I don't have the money. I can't get twenty dollars.' Rick exploded into his face. 'Find it,' he hissed and shoved him in the shoulders. Trembling, Jamie gathered his breath and said, 'I don't even want a knife.' and pushed his way around Rick, running for the street. As he ran he heard Rick yelling behind him, 'Friday! I want it all by Friday!' He knew now that they weren't going to leave him alone.

"For the next two days he stayed in the cafeteria all through lunch, skulked through the halls between classes and, when the last bell rang, he took off out of the school's back door, running for home. He still hadn't told anyone about the harassment and he honestly thought that his only option was to hide. It didn't do any good though. When Friday came, they were waiting for him as he ran out the back door. Rick stepped in front of him and said, 'You owe me twenty bucks.' 'I don't want the knife, and I don't have the money,' Jamie replied. Rick shoved Jamie in the chest and said, 'You don't have a choice.' Jamie stumbled back a step and looked around for a way out, but the other kids were closing in on him. Stepping towards him, Rick shoved Jamie again and said, 'I want the money.' Jamie was getting frantic. For a third time, Rick moved close to Jamie and pushed him hard. It hurt. Without thinking, Jamie threw his arms out and pushed Rick away from him. Suddenly everyone stood still. The kids all looked at Rick. They were waiting to see what he would do. For a second Rick looked nervous, eyes darting around the circle of kids. Jamie thought Rick might let him go. Instead, Rick punched him in the ribs.

"Jamie collapsed onto the pavement and Rick and the others started kicking him in the back and in the stomach. They left him crying and struggling for breath. After they left, Jamie dragged himself to his feet, stumbled to his locker for another T-shirt from his gym bag and then went to the washroom to clean himself up. By the time he was finished he looked fairly normal, like he'd just been playing soccer. Before he left the school he telephoned his parents and told them he'd stayed late for a practice.

"When he got home, his parents told him to get ready for dinner. But Jamie was too upset to eat. He sat at the table, staring at his plate and feeling his stomach tighten every time he thought about school. Unfortunately the pain in his side where they'd hit him wouldn't let him forget. It bothered him all weekend. By Sunday evening, he was worried sick. He spent another sleepless night rolling around in his bed, driving himself crazy with fear. In the morning his eyes were red and swollen. He looked awful, even worse than he had earlier in the week, and his mother was worried enough to ask if he was sick. But when he just shook his head sullenly, she hurried him out the door to school.

"Jamie didn't make it to school. Rick and the others met him as he turned the corner onto a street two blocks away. Without even asking for the money they ran at him and the first ones to reach him grabbed at his arms. Jamie screamed and struggled but they pinned him again and for the second time punched and kicked at his ribs and stomach until it hurt to breathe. Two of his ribs were broken, but at that moment all he knew was that he needed to get away. Instead of going into the school to report what had happened to the principal or a teacher, he ran back towards home.

"For the next three days he managed to stay home, in bed, not eating or even talking much. His parents thought it was the flu. He couldn't stay home forever though and on the Friday he reluctantly returned to school. Nothing happened on the way there and when nobody bothered him all day, he began to feel a little better. He thought that maybe Rick had moved on to somebody else – forgotten about him. But it didn't last.

"After school, he went down the front steps, trying to stay with groups of other kids. But as he passed the parking lot, he saw Rick and the other guys leaning on the wall beside the gym doors. Rick shouted when he saw Jamie trailing behind a group of older kids. Immediately Rick's small gang took off after Jamie. He ran across the road and then turned right onto the main street. A few doors down was a convenience store that most of the kids went to during lunch or after school. Jamie tore through the door and ran to the counter screaming at the women working there as Rick and two others burst in close behind him. As the kids grabbed Jamie's coat and arms, pulling him towards the door, Jamie shouted at the women, screaming for help. As they forced open the door and shoved Jamie through it, the store owner picked up the phone and dialed 911.

"That was when the police got involved. Rick was placed in custody and charged with assault. That's all I'm going to tell you for now. Why don't we take a break and when we regroup we'll talk about the three most important points to understand about youth violence."

2

THE 3 MOST IMPORTANT POINTS TO UNDERSTAND ABOUT YOUTH VIOLENCE

I held up my hands to get everyone's attention. "Okay," I said, "in this second half, what I really want to cover is the three most important points to understand about youth violence.

"Number one – Our kids are growing up in a radically different world. Number two – The Violence Ladder: the escalation from simple harassment to full-fledged violence. And, Number three – Parents can help protect their kids.

"These are the three basic things that you need to know about kids and crime. They're based on what I have seen and heard while working on the streets and talking to children at their schools. As we go through those points in more detail, I'll draw on the story about Rick and Jamie that I just told you for examples and if you have any questions, don't hesitate to ask.

POINT 1: OUR KIDS ARE GROWING UP IN A RADICALLY DIFFERENT WORLD

"You know," I began, "after beating up Jamie, Rick was arrested and charged with assault. But when I went to visit his parents, to try to find out what was going on with their son, Rick's father became very defensive. When I told him that Rick had threatened and assaulted another kid, even broke two of his ribs, he just shrugged and said, 'Oh come on, Rick was just hanging around with his friends. They're kids. I'm sure it was just an accident.'

"It's not the first time I've heard something like that. Many other parents that I talk to say things like, 'Well, you know, it's just a phase. . . he's a teenager.' Or, 'I did the same stuff when I was a kid.' But that's just not true.

"I speak to your kids everyday and they tell me things they probably aren't telling anybody else, especially their parents. They tell me that there are kids in their schools who carry weapons to class, that some kids group together into gangs for protection, and that only a very small minority of children are violent or aggressive. Today, our sons and daughters fear for their safety, and that is a change from when I was in school fifteen years ago.

A SMALL PERCENTAGE OF KIDS ARE A LARGE PART OF THE PROBLEM

"Dr. Fred Mathews, a community psychologist at Central Toronto Youth Services and a teacher in the graduate school of the University of Toronto, points out in a study called *The Badge & The Book* that there is a small core of violent kids out there – about 5% of all children – who commit most of the hard-core crimes. But, what is markedly different from 30 years ago is the fact that in recent years, there has been a tremendous growth in the number of kids who are on the edge. This is the group, maybe 20-30% of all children, who may not be bad kids looking for trouble like Rick – but are just bored and restless. These kids are easily swayed by pressure from others and are naturally attracted to guys like Rick. These are the kids who supported Rick in the confrontation with Jamie. They're the ones who formed a circle around Rick, urged him on when it looked like things would become violent, and then jumped in and helped assault Jamie."

In the back of the classroom I saw a woman's hand go up. "Hi, Kevin, my name's Jackie. I can see your point that there are a few bad eggs out there causing most of the trouble, but I've never heard of any gangs at this school. So when you tell us that there's a whole group of kids in our schools who are good, maybe from decent homes and yet they end up in serious trouble, or a gang, or whatever, I find that hard to believe. Why would those kids do that? I mean, I just don't get it."

At the front of the room I nodded and thought for a second. Jackie's reaction wasn't an unusual one. Many people have a hard time believing that so many kids can make mistakes or bad decisions and end up involved in a criminal act with a kid like Rick.

"Jackie," I said, "let me walk you through how Rick became a ringleader for those other kids. That should help you understand what motivates kids to step over the line and join in a criminal activity – even if they would never intend that to happen.

Kids get something important out of being in a gang

"What you need to understand about Rick is that he was a new kid at that school, but he very quickly attracted a circle of kids around him because he had an attitude and wasn't afraid to cause trouble. He had the same attitude and behaved like characters they saw in movies or videos. That made him cool. So it's not surprising that kids would want to hang around with him and try to earn his respect.

"This is especially true of kids who don't have a strong sense of themselves. They aren't sure enough about who they are and what they stand for to carve their own path and make their own friends so they copy what they see on TV or start hanging out with a kid like Rick.

"You see, joining a gang like the one that Rick led actually has a lot of benefits for a young kid. It's hard for us to think of the problem this way, but you have to realize kids wouldn't join gangs unless there was something in it for them.

"When I sit in a classroom or an office, alone with a boy who has been caught committing a crime I always hear the same story. Typically, these kids have low self-esteem, problems at home or few friends. They're basically unhappy. They have no confidence in themselves or the people around them. They don't feel they can make a difference which makes them susceptible to bullies or gangs. They end up making bad choices when faced with difficult situations because they don't feel they have anywhere to turn.

"I can't tell you the number of kids who break down in front of me. I'm talking about tough kids who have been arrested for assault or worse. When I finally get through to them and get them to tell me why they hit somebody or stole something – I usually find out that they feel like they are completely alone. Powerless. When they get to that point they either became victims – or they strike back. They band together or join a gang. If you think back to the story I told, you can see how Rick and his friends stuck together for power, protection, and a sense of self-worth.

"Also, many victims are loners and they turn to gangs not only for the protection they afford, but also for the friendship. We are conditioned to look at gangs as dysfunctional, criminal organizations, and they are. But to a young kid there are many benefits to being in a gang like Rick's, such as increased self-esteem and a feeling of importance. For the first time in their lives, many of them receive respect from other students, simply because they are in a gang. Small kids suddenly feel huge and strong because they have the power of a large group. When I talk to them, many say that the gang is like a family to them. They take from it the things they may not be getting from their actual family at home.

"My point is kids don't join gangs to mess up their lives, they join them to improve their lives. This, of course, doesn't make sense from an adult, outsider perspective but it does if we get inside their heads, and inside their world. What looks like chaos and mayhem from the outside actually has an internal logic. And the key to breaking the escalation of gang activity is figuring out that logic and attacking it appropriately.

"I think one of the biggest problems we have right now is that 'reactive policing' – that is arresting criminals and throwing them in jail – doesn't solve the original problem of why kids join gangs in the first place. No matter how many times we react and punish criminals who are members of gangs, we won't eliminate the problem because the kids will still have the same needs: security, friendship and status. And they'll continue to group together to meet those needs if they can't be met anywhere else.

"In some way, an escalation in the number of arrests that we make could even strengthen those attitudes. As their lives become more unstable I'm sure they would have an even greater need to protect each other from the police."

At the back of the room I saw a man raise a hand. "My name's Robert," he said. "I don't personally agree with what you said about reactive policing or whatever you call it. I think we need harsher sentences and more police, if anything. But, I don't want to argue this point now. I would like to know how a bully in our school today is different than a guy who was a bully twenty years ago?"

15

THE SAFETY OF A GROUP MAKES KIDS BEHAVE MORE AGGRESSIVELY

"As far as school-yard bullying is concerned," I said, "you can see the difference between 1975 and 1996 if you compare what you remember from your own childhood to what happened to Jamie. Today, bullies rarely act alone. It's not a case of big kids picking on smaller kids so much as it is groups of kids picking on loners. What Rick and his friends did to Jamie is now typical of bullying incidents.

"The days of the single bully are over. As I've said, there are no longer any one-on-one fights in the school yard. Being a bully has always been about having an unfair advantage that allows you to dominate weaker people, and that domination is what gives the bully the thrill. It's a power game. But these days the only way to have power and exert control over others in the school yard or on the streets is by being part of a group or carrying a weapon that you're willing to use."

At that point a hand went up. "My name's Ian. This sounds to me like the swarmings that we hear about on the news. You know, where a bunch of kids attack somebody on the street and steal their jacket or shoes or wallet. How is that different than what you're talking about?"

"Actually, it's not that different, Ian," I answered. "The same impulses and desires are motivating the kids in both scenarios. There was a study done recently by Dr. Fred Mathews that looked at why violence occurs. Through interviews with many offenders and victims, he established that it's all about control and power, and has nothing to do with the need for the material objects that are stolen, like the jacket or the wallet. The kids who do the swarming do it for the "high" they get seeing fear on the face of the victim. It's a pure rush for them, and to me that's frightening."

I stopped for a second to let that sink in, looked around the room and then asked, "Any other questions about understanding the world our kids live in and how, or why, it has changed in the past few years?"

A woman in the corner of the room spoke up. "Hi, Kevin. My name's Mary," she started. "I'm just still not sure that this is as big a problem as you're making it out to be. Like Jackie said, I haven't heard of trouble at this school, and you've really only focused on the one story. I guess I just want to understand the magnitude of the problem."

"Well, Mary," I replied, "I don't want to get into stats at this point because I want you to see how individual kids become victims. Telling you about the violent crime rate at this point probably wouldn't have much meaning and wouldn't help you solve the problem. We'll be covering the stats in detail in a couple months. So, for now, I'll try to illustrate what I'm talking about with more concrete examples.

THERE IS MORE YOUTH VIOLENCE THAN EVER BEFORE

"Today a simple insult can result in a knife being pulled, and a serious crime being committed. This past summer for instance I dealt with a classroom incident in East Toronto in which a grade seven student was stabbed in the throat with a ball-point pen just because he was teasing the kid beside him. Last month, in a high school in my neighbourhood a student was stabbed with a broken bottle in a stairwell and needed 37 stitches. The victim hadn't done anything wrong.

"When we were kids, bullies used to throw snowballs, or push kids to the ground and stuff grass or snow down their clothing. Today, our kids are being hurt by broken glass that is being stuffed inside a snowball. And instead of being humiliated by an ice-cold handful of snow down their shirts, our children are being seriously injured by groups of kids kicking at their ribs while they're down on the ground.

"Just to put it in perspective for you, imagine if you had to go to the office worried that a co-worker might shoot you because of an argument over the photocopier or if you had to worry that the woman checking out produce at the supermarket was carrying a knife in her purse. It has become that strange and sad.

"The physical results of violence are undeniably terrible, but the psychological damage is immeasurable. Kids who don't suffer physical violence may still suffer mentally. Terror, shame, and guilt can make life miserable for many kids. The important thing is to put yourself in your child's mind – walk through a typical day with them and think about everything they are exposed to, and you'll see how hard it is for them." I stopped for a second and looked around the room. The faces in front of me were stiff and unsmiling. "I've been talking for awhile," I said, "Why don't you give me your input?"

Near the front of the class a woman said, "Hi, my name's Lydia. I guess, Kevin, you've just been doing your lectures and talking to kids in

Metro Toronto. I'm sure you've done research across the country, but it seems to me these problems are cropping up everywhere, not just in Toronto. I heard a story this summer from my dad and it made me think that, even if we don't believe we have a problem now, we could have one eventually. He told me about a conversation that he had with my four-teen-year-old niece – she's a shy girl, who's on the honour roll in a high school in a small suburb of Calgary.

"She said to my dad matter-of-factly, 'Oh, I know a guy in my class who carries a knife. Everybody knows somebody. . . .' Needless to say he was shocked. He asked her how that made her feel, and she said, 'I don't know, scared I guess. But that's just how it is. What can I do about it?'"

"Yeah, that's a story I hear a lot," I said shaking my head. "I think a lot of parents are surprised though, when they find out what is going on in their children's schools. I guess I've spent the last little while telling you how many kids are involved in violent crime. But I would like to strong-ly reiterate, before we move on to my second point, that most kids are good. Most kids are not going to run out and commit a crime this year. In fact, if anything, most kids stand a much higher chance of becoming a victim than an offender."

I looked at the clock and saw that we only had twenty minutes remaining. "Okay," I said, "we went pretty deep on that point and we're running out of time, so what I'd like to do is briefly talk about the last two of the most important points you need to understand about youth violence as they relate to Rick and Jamie's story.

"Those two points deal with the Violence Ladder and how parents can help protect their kids. Let's start with the Violence Ladder."

POINT 2: THE VIOLENCE LADDER — FIVE STEPS

"In my experience, although I do come across random violence – violence out of nowhere — a lot of the violence that I see kids involved in can be explained in terms of what I call the Violence Ladder. The Violence Ladder is an easy-to-remember phrase that illustrates the escalation from relatively insignificant acts like teasing or name calling into full-blown criminal behaviour. Whereas random violence is something that will always be difficult to prevent, violence that results from the Violence Ladder is much more preventable. So, when we talk about violence over the next several months we will be focusing our attention on the Violence Ladder, because a real opportunity to protect our kids lies in breaking the Violence Ladder.

"In my view, there are five basic steps on the Violence Ladder: harassment, threats, grouping, weapons, and serious violence. For our purposes, when I say harassment I mean low-level harassment such as when one kid calls another kid an idiot, or gives him the finger, or bumps into him in the hall. By threats, I mean something more serious, like when one kid tells another kid he's gonna beat him up, or stab him. Grouping is when kids gang up on a single kid or take on another gang. Weapons, of course, speaks for itself – that's when a weapon is introduced into the equation. Either a kid brandishes a weapon, or uses it to injure somebody. Serious violence is the last step in this series of events. These steps aren't carved in stone anywhere, and sometimes a step is skipped every now and then, but they do illustrate a basic pattern – a pattern that I have personally witnessed countless times. And as we will see in the story I just told you about Jamie and Rick, and in the stories I'm going to tell you in the coming months, there are many ways to move up the five steps of the Violence Ladder.

"Sometimes it takes months to go from harassment all the way to serious violence, other times it takes only minutes. Sometimes an already established group is responsible for the initial harassment, other times a completely new group forms as a result of the harassment. The main point about the Violence Ladder is the simple fact that when you see one step, like harassment, the next steps are bound to follow. You don't just get one kid harassing another and that's the end of it. Once the escalation has started it continues. And too often it continues all the way to its conclusion of serious violence. Unlike random violence, which is unpredictable, you can see the violence escalate up the Violence Ladder. This is a critical point – if you see the initial steps in the Violence Ladder occurring you have the opportunity to step in and break it.

"Fortunately for Jamie, his version of the Violence Ladder skipped the step involving a weapon – but remember, the promise of a weapon – a knife – was what instigated the climb from harassment to violence.

STEP 1: HARASSMENT

"If you remember, Jamie was crossing the school yard alone after school and stumbled across Rick and his friends. They were just hanging out, not necessarily looking for someone to beat up. They saw a lone guy walking across the empty playground and thought they'd have some fun. And, although they hadn't planned to harass Jamie, this was a classic first step up the Violence Ladder.

"From that point on, things began to escalate and all of the kids involved lost control over the situation. Jamie didn't report the initial incident to the school staff – he didn't even tell his parents about it. That's a big mistake, but I will talk about that when we cover point number three – parents can help protect their kids.

STEP 2: THREATS

"Instead of telling his parents about Rick, Jamie decided to stand up to the group, telling Rick that he didn't have the money and didn't want the knife they were supposedly selling. At this point, Rick climbed another rung in the ladder and threatened Jamie, saying that he'd better have the money by Friday or else. You can see how Rick had now trapped himself. By issuing an ultimatum to Jamie, he had committed himself to action in front of his gang – if Jamie didn't pay, Rick would be forced to follow through on his threat to save face in front of the others.

STEP 3: GROUPING

"After the harassment and the threats, Rick and his friends started working together as a tight unit. This type of cooperation is called grouping. When they met Jamie for the third time they surrounded him. Rick began shoving Jamie around, hoping the more serious threat from the entire group would scare him enough to make him pay.

STEP 4: WEAPONS

"In this case, although a knife was the excuse for the initial harassment, no weapon was actually produced. However, we will see in upcoming stories that weapons are often involved and the violence that results is much more serious.

STEP 5: VIOLENCE

"After Rick pushed Jamie, Jamie pushed back. Instantly all eyes in the group focused on Rick. His reputation was on the line. Initially, all he'd wanted was twenty dollars from Jamie and no trouble. Now he was forced to defend his position as a tough guy. It was never any contest. Rick hit Jamie and then the other kids joined in – just to confirm their commitment to the group and to be able to share in the feeling of power that Rick held over a helpless victim.

"That was a very quick example of the Violence Ladder and what I'd like to do is hold your questions about it until our next meeting. I'd like to start that meeting off with a much more serious story that better illustrates the escalation of violent behaviour. You can bring all of your questions to that meeting. For now, I'd just like to move on to the third most important thing to understand about youth violence: that there is hope and that parents can do something about the problem. I think it's important that you leave here tonight with at least one concrete solution you can put into effect within your own families."

POINT 3: PARENTS CAN HELP PROTECT THEIR KIDS

I leaned on the desk and looked around at the parents. "A lot of the solutions we will discuss in the course of our monthly meetings will focus on the idea of breaking the Violence Ladder, and the earlier you break the Violence Ladder, the better. However, we should try our best to prevent the escalation of violence from ever happening in the first place. . . . As I mentioned before, I think the biggest mistake Jamie made during that whole two week ordeal was the fact that he didn't tell anybody what was happening to him – not his friends, his parents or the school staff. Had he reported the initial incident when Rick was merely harassing him, the Violence Ladder would have been broken. But he didn't. And that's why this story is a perfect example of how kids can make themselves a victim.

"So, tonight I'd like you to consider the following question: how could Jamie's parents have prevented the violence their child experienced?

"The reason I'm asking you what Jamie's parents could have done instead of just giving you my answer is that you're all parents yourselves. You all have children that go to this school and that means they must be at least 5 years old, but my son Torin is only six months old. Although I spend everyday talking to kids of all ages I just don't have the parenting experience that you all have. So, it wouldn't seem right to me, if I just tried to force my solutions down your throat. Instead, I'd like to get your input and then together we can develop some solutions."

As I finished speaking I looked to my right and saw Mary's hand go up. "I'm not really sure what I would have done," she said, "but how did Jamie's parents react?"

"Jamie's parents were shocked, absolutely stunned when they found out what had been happening for so long," I replied. "They found it almost impossible to believe that they didn't notice that something was wrong. I think that Jamie's parents, as well as being angry with Rick and the others, felt upset with themselves. I think, in retrospect, they realized the changes in Jamie's behaviour should have been a tip-off that something was very wrong. And there are definite warning signs that shouldn't be ignored. In a few months we'll be spending an entire session on what signs parents should watch out for, but for now, let me point out Jamie's sudden loss of appetite, his unusual hours at school, the state of his clothes and hygiene when he returned home at night, the fact that he spoke little, became sullen and withdrawn: these are all clear indicators that something significant is occurring in a child's life."

A woman spoke up and said, "Hi, I'm Wendy, Ian's wife. What Kevin just said makes sense to me. In a case like this though, don't you think he would tell somebody? Especially his parents, his own mother? I just can't believe that my son wouldn't tell me."

"We would all like to think they would tell us anything," I said. "But, you have to put yourself in their shoes for a moment. I often talk to them after they have been beaten up, harassed or robbed, and they're usually dealing with a lot of very powerful and very confusing emotions. They may be angry, ashamed and afraid. And, specifically they may be afraid of retaliation from the offenders, they may be afraid of getting friends into trouble, or of being thought of as a rat by their classmates. They may also be afraid that they won't be believed or that parents, school authorities or police won't take them seriously and won't act on the problem.

"Especially in their teenage years they don't want to be seen by others at their school as being friendless, or vulnerable. I've even had kids tell me that they didn't report an assault because they were afraid their parents would be angry that their clothes were ripped. And what's important about that is, it doesn't really matter whether their parents actually would have been angry – I can't see how anybody would be if their child was hurt

– but it's the kids' perception of the situation that keeps them from reporting a crime. If a crime isn't reported, things get worse not better."

At that moment Wendy spoke up. "I guess it's important for us to tell our kids that they have to report harassment or threats to somebody," she said. "I think we need to be absolutely clear about that. That means sitting down with our kids and explaining this issue to them – even using the story about Rick and Jamie – if it helps to clarify what we're saying. It's not good enough to just assume that because they're seven or ten or fifteen that they necessarily know how important it is to report all incidents like that. And maybe they don't understand the consequences. I mean, just look at what happened to Jamie – it can be really dangerous for our kids if they don't tell us or a teacher or the police."

"Exactly, Wendy," I said. "They have to tell somebody. Otherwise the escalation of violence will continue. That's one of the reasons that Rick was pushed to act so aggressively – he knew that Jamie wasn't going to turn him in and so he was able to keep pushing and pushing until violence erupted. Actually, the story that you'll hear next month is an even more serious example of what can happen when kids don't report harassing or threatening behaviour. What happened to the victim in that case is frightening."

When I'd finished talking, I saw Lydia raise her hand. "Kevin," she began, "if we're telling our kids to talk to us – to report everything – isn't it really important that we listen carefully. I know I make a real effort to focus on my kids when they're telling me about their day. I show how interested I am by asking questions – getting them to reveal more about what was happening to them. I find that really helps."

"Yes, that's key," I said. "You know, when I speak to children I ask them how we can help. And they say – I wish somebody would just listen. It's as simple as that. And as I travel from school to school, the most positive reaction I get is that they are surprised that someone is listening. So, based on that, my advice would be don't leave them alone out there. Ask them about their friends, meet their friends' parents, find out who they are going out with at night and where. Who else is hanging around? How dangerous do you think it is? How safe do they think they are? What makes them scared? Get informed and then you can help them.

SUMMARY

"Okay," I said, "before we call a close to this meeting I'd like to quickly summarize the three most important points to understand about youth violence. One – our children are growing up in a world that is radically different than the one we grew up in. It is more violent and stressful. So, when your child comes to you with a problem, don't interpret what they're going through in terms of what it was like when you were their age. Two – there is a Violence Ladder in which harassment escalates to threats to grouping to carrying weapons and finally to serious violence. And three – parents can help protect their kids. Specifically, we said that we have to encourage our children to report any harassment, threats or violent behaviour.

"I would like to finish by giving you a quick preview of where we're going from here. Over the next seven months we'll be learning as much as we can about the problem of youth violence. Each time we meet, I'll tell you a story that helps illustrate our three main points. Until the end of the year, we will focus mainly on the first two points, and then after that we'll concentrate on our third point – how to prevent our kids from becoming victims.

"In the next three meetings, every story I tell you will make clear how things are different and will be a good example of the Violence Ladder. The Violence Ladder will also lead us into an in-depth discussion of gangs. We'll learn how kids come together to form gangs, why they act so violently, and the difference between male and female gangs. We'll tie everything together by looking at the statistics which will reveal how serious the problem of youth violence has become in Canada over the past few years."

PART 2

The Violence Ladder

3

VIOLENCE RUINS
A GOOD KID'S LIFE

When I arrived at the classroom for our October meeting everyone was already settled in their seats. I walked over to the teacher's desk and welcomed them all back.

"Last month, I mentioned I would start with another story, this time one that ended rather badly. It's about a good kid who winds up committing a horrible crime. From it, we'll learn quite a bit about our first two points – how things are different today, and how the Violence Ladder works. And we'll touch on the third point as well – how we as parents can help protect our kids.

"This story is a perfect example of how pressure from classmates or the cool, tough, troublemaking minority can cause a well-behaved kid to go wrong. In fact, this story is similar to the story I told you at our first meeting. It's a variation on a theme. In the first story, Rick, the instigator, wanted to have some fun and maybe score twenty bucks in the process. However, in this story, the instigators have a much deeper, more wicked motive. And there's another key difference: here, there really is a knife.

CHRIS'S STORY

"This incident happened a couple of years ago, and at the time, I was working at a division in the east end. It was a fairly slow spring afternoon around the station when I got a call from a youth whose voice I didn't recognize. He sounded like he was about seventeen or so. He croaked hello, barely able to get the words out, and then clammed up.

"I introduced myself as 'P.C. Guest' and then waited for him to speak, but the line remained quiet. I could hear breathing, fast and shallow, and an occasional pop or click from the open line. In the background, I could hear a woman's strong voice calling, but couldn't make out what she was saying. The kid couldn't find any words, which was normal, I guess, because teenagers don't spend a lot of time talking to people like me.

"'Do you want me to talk to your mother?' I asked. 'I can hear her back there.' At the time, I remember thinking that he might have just had his bike stolen, or been in a fight. But when he eventually spoke I realized it was much more serious.

"'No! No,' he said quickly, in a panic. 'She doesn't know anything about this. And I don't want her to know, okay.'

"'Sure,' I said, 'but that means you're gonna have to tell me what's going on and I need to start with your name and where you live.'

"He stammered that his name was Chris and went on to say, 'I don't want to go to jail, sir. I don't want my mom. . . she would kill me. I'm supposed to be going to university in the fall, I just finished my exams. I don't know who to talk to. . . . I don't want to hurt her. . . .'

"He wouldn't tell me over the phone what it was he had done. I remember that I just tried to make my voice warm and sympathetic. He was obviously afraid. From experience I would have bet that he hadn't slept in days. I'd have been surprised if he'd eaten. And it sounded like he was all alone with whatever guilt he was feeling. I wondered what his parents thought was wrong. Perhaps they figured he was just sick. I tried to imagine what he was going through. Kids call the police when they figure they've got nowhere else to turn. When the people they thought were friends don't care, when their folks aren't around, or aren't listening or would fly into a fury if they told them. I was anxious to know what he'd done. After all, he had said he was going to university and we don't get college-bound kids calling to confess to big crimes everyday.

"Finally his nerves started to smooth themselves out and he eventually managed to tell me where he lived.

"'Chris, I want you to tell me what happened,' I said to him as I wrote down his address. 'But I want you to know you can trust me, okay? I don't know what you've done, but calling here was the right thing to do. Why don't you give me the details?'

"'It's the subway stabbing,' he said shakily.

"I put my pen down and paused for a second. I was stunned because that had been a big case, and everyone was talking about it. I can remember that I suddenly got very excited. A lot of these tips don't lead us anywhere, but it seemed like this kid was telling me he did it, and that thought made me close my eyes for a second. Even after five years on the service and God knows how many of these cases I'd seen, it still felt awful.

"Two days before, a mob of youths had overrun one of the subway cars, which isn't all that unusual these days. Witnesses said they were all around seventeen years old, wearing new baggy jeans and baseball caps. They were pushing and shoving each other, swearing and threatening the people sitting near them, quickly spreading to fill the whole car like they owned it. It had been hard for the officers who investigated to get a good description of what had happened as the car moved from station to station, because most of the business travelers had gotten off the train or changed cars as soon as they could. But it didn't sound like the kind of situation a college-bound kid who called you 'sir' would find himself in. It was more like typical gang activity.

"All we knew was that at one of the stops the crowd suddenly swelled. More kids piled in. There was a lot of shouting, and fighting broke out. Someone screamed and the car emptied. The officer's report described how, on the floor, curled around one of the metal upright poles was a thin kid in big basketball shoes. His lips drawn back, teeth clenched, eyes closed. Blood stained his T-shirt.

"There had been a few witnesses to the melee. But none of them had seen the stabbing. The officers investigating the case had spoken to the victim later at the hospital. He had a mess of stitches and wouldn't be playing basketball for a few months. But he was tight-lipped. He said he had no idea who did it, or why. The victim was probably more afraid of his own gang friends than of Chris, the kid who'd cut him up.

"Based on the few identifications that the other passengers had provided, the officers had been able to work out which gangs were involved. The gang members were well known to everyone in the station from drug busts, assault, petty thefts. But that was a dead end as well. None of them would step outside the group, risk being labeled untrustworthy or disciplined for talking. That wasn't strange, it happens all the time, in all kinds of situations. The same kind of pressures exist in any group.

"Stabbing meant assault. Even for a first offense, the kid was probably looking at two years in a correctional facility. Not exactly the Harvard he had hoped for.

"Over the phone, Chris told me that he wanted to tell me all about it. He asked me to come and pick him up.

"As I drove to Chris's apartment with my partner, I thought about how strange it was that he was involved in a gang problem like this. He certainly didn't fit the profile. Gang members don't call into the station to confess, and they don't usually graduate and go on to university. Even Chris's apartment was in a nice building, in a nice neighbourhood, near a park in the suburb. It wasn't even in my division.

"The low-rise apartment where Chris lived was planted between rows of old brick homes. The whole neighbourhood had been put up back in the twenties. As I parked the car, my partner and I exchanged glances. There was no need to say anything, we both knew what the other was thinking. Here we were in a decent part of town about to arrest a decent kid for a very indecent crime. Twenty years ago this was unheard of. Ten years ago it was unusual. Now we do it every week. It's true that the typical inner city crimes – break-ins, car theft, drugs, assault – have been bleeding into the rest of the city at an alarming rate.

"When we knocked on the door of Chris's apartment, his younger brother answered. We asked for Chris and his brother's eyes went wide. I'll never forget the look of panic on his face when he realized that the police had come for his brother. He screamed for his mother. He could only have been about eleven or twelve.

"Chris beat his mom to the door by about two seconds, immediately trying to push us into the hall, but his mother grabbed him and pulled him back into the apartment. She asked us if something was wrong. Behind her I could see Chris panicking. I told his mother we were there to talk to Chris about an assault at the subway station two nights ago. 'A boy was stabbed. He's in the hospital,' I said to her.

"'What would Chris know about that?' she said. I remember seeing her face wrinkling in confusion. But underneath I could see suspicion and a layer of sadness. I knew she didn't want to believe.

"I told her that Chris had called us about an hour before and said that he knew what happened. I suggested we come inside and talk about it.

"We went over to a large couch. I saw piles of school books at each end of it. As we sat down, Chris's mother turned to him and asked what all this was about. She wanted to know what he knew about a boy being stabbed.

"Beside her, Chris put his head down and covered his face with his hands. I saw him starting to shake. His mother asked him whether it was true that he had called us. Nervously, Chris told her, 'Ma, it was me. I did it.' He explained how he couldn't tell her that he had stabbed that kid, and that he didn't even know him.

"After that Chris threw himself into her shoulder.

"His mother started to cry and turned to look at us. I remember standing awkwardly beside my partner with my book out and pen in hand. She said, 'Chris has never been in any trouble, officer. What happened? He just finished school. What happened?!'

"'I don't know,' I told her. I said that we needed Chris to come down to the station with us. He'd just confessed to a very serious crime and I was going to have to read him his rights. I told his mother that she should meet us down there.

"I watched, feeling awful as she screamed, 'No, no, not Chris.'

"We drove back to the station in silence. Most of the people we carry in the cruiser under arrest are mean and unrepentant. They kick and bang the plexiglass barrier. But Chris just sat slumped in the back seat, his head bowed. In the rear-view mirror, I could see his shoulders heaving slightly. I felt a lot of pity for him and I was anxious to find out how he ended up in this situation.

"At the station, I led him into a small interview room, offered him a seat in a wooden chair and sat down across from him. I told him to relax and said that his mother was outside. I asked him to tell me what happened. I can still picture him now. How small and skinny and scared he looked. His eyes were red from crying. What a shame that a kid like this did what he did.

"Over the next half hour, Chris told me the whole story in detail. Three days before, he'd been approached between classes by a guy he barely knew. Chris went to a local high school that had about twelve hundred kids. This kid wasn't in any of Chris's classes and the only thing he really knew about him was that his nickname was Stick. He pulled Chris aside in the crowded hallway. Chris told me how his huge leather jacket smelled like marijuana smoke. Stick said that a guy from another school had it in for him. 'He's gonna kill ya, man,' Stick told him. 'But we talked him down. We told him he doesn't want to do that.'

"Chris told me he was scared to death. 'What? Who?' he asked Stick. 'Why does he want to kill me? I don't even know him.'

"'I know,' said Stick. 'Mistaken identity, wrong guy. We told him. But he needs to see you to make sure.'

"Chris was terrified, but said that he felt relieved that at least someone was there to look out for him, especially someone that hardly knew him. Chris told me that Stick and his friends were the cool students. They were a little bit older, and had a bit of a reputation as troublemakers. They were the guys who were always outside smoking, laughing with the girls, or getting into fights. They were standing up for Chris. He felt like he belonged for the first time in five years.

"Stick told Chris they would all go with him to take care of the problem. He said, 'Tonight, after school we'll meet this kid that wants to get you at the subway and we'll talk it out.'

"So, after school, Chris met Stick and seven other guys. They made their way to the subway and got on a train. Everyone except Chris was pretty loud, yelling and screaming at the other passengers, hitting each other, kidding around. They kept chucking Chris on the arm, telling him to lighten up. It was going to be fine. They were taking care of him. Chris said it felt great. He was anxious, alright, but he was also excited.

"After two stops, another half dozen kids he didn't recognize got on and came over to face them. They were swearing at him and Stick and the others, banging sticks against the steel poles.

"Stick turned to Chris and said, 'That guy over there, the one with the Jordan's and the red jacket, he's the guy that wants you.' Suddenly the two groups met, everyone was grabbing for someone, guys were falling down, punching and kicking. The other commuters shrank back in fear. Chris was frozen in the middle of the chaos. He felt somebody pass him something. He looked down, in his hand was a knife. He'd never held one before. It was a four inch razor-sharp blade.

"'Do it!' somebody screamed. 'He's right in front of you. . . .'

"Chris saw the red jacket charging at him and squeezed his eyes shut tight.

"At the next stop, the two gangs unloaded from the car, and disappeared out of the subway station. The terrified commuters ran alongside them. Chris stood in the middle of the empty car, the knife in his hand. On the floor at his feet a young boy was squirming, clutching his back. Someone had hit the panic alarm and the train was stalled. Half a minute passed. Still no one came. Chris took one last look at the kid and ran out of the station, onto a bus, and went home.

"That was Chris's story. He was breathing heavily. He asked for his mom. But I still had some questions. He had given me a decent description of Stick, but I needed to know about the other kids. He told me as much as he could. Then I asked him what he did with the knife. And then I asked him why he did it.

"He told me he didn't know. He had been confused, didn't know what the right thing to do was. Everything seemed so unreal he said – Stick, the threat, the gangs, and then the knife. Someone yelled for him to do it, so he did. Simple as that.

"If the reality of his actions hadn't sunk in by the time he called to turn himself in, things certainly took shape at that point, as he sat face to face with a police officer from the Street Crime Unit, under arrest.

"I asked Chris about his career at school. I expected a failing average, absences, the usual kid stuff. But the past year he'd been getting B's, and had just finished his final exams. A couple of weeks before he'd received acceptance letters to three Ontario universities: York, Brock and Trent. His mother had been so proud.

"Hearing this really bothered me. Here was a perfectly good student who had just flushed his bright future down the toilet. I had seen similar cases in the past few months, and they always really affect me. Like those others, Chris wasn't your basic criminal. He was both a victim and an offender. He was a good kid who somehow had been driven to commit a violent crime, to puncture a stranger's kidney for no good reason.

"A few weeks later, Chris's case went before a judge. He pleaded guilty and was sentenced to one year in youth detention. He ended up taking correspondence courses, and his future is certainly far less bright than it used to be. Chris's mom never really got over what happened. She moved and doesn't leave the house much anymore. Chris's brother changed schools and spends all of his time studying."

I looked around at the faces of the parents. They looked somber, quiet. I suggested we all take ten.

THESE GANG KIDS ARE SMART

After the break, we looked at Chris's story in light of the three most important points to understand about youth violence. "As for our first point – our kids are growing up in a radically different world," I said, "there's a few things I want to point out. First of all, there's the obvious – the fact that Chris is not the type of person that comes to mind when we conjure up the image of a violent criminal. When tragedies like this one spread throughout the community, or hit the press, we're all shocked. It doesn't make sense. How does a good kid turn bad like that, so quickly, so drastically? But, if you take a closer look at what happened it's not so surprising. In fact, it makes a lot of sense. The instigators, Stick and his gang, had devised a very subtle plan, and executed it expertly. I think that's a major thing for us adults to understand about kids and violence today – that troublemakers are so much more sophisticated. The fact is, we're not dealing with simple thugs, we're up against scheming criminals. Kids like Stick know how to spot vulnerable kids, and they know exactly how to manipulate situations to their advantage. That's what's different – in their own way, these gang kids are smart."

At that point Robert spoke up. "Kevin, it sounds to me like you're making excuses for Chris. I feel sorry for the kid, sure, but what he did was plain wrong. He made the choice. He did it all on his own."

"You're right. I don't disagree with you one bit. In fact, one of the things I really impress upon the kids when I speak to them is this idea of choice. But a lot of kids don't feel they have a choice. They get in too deep, and lose their perspective. That's what happened to Chris. I'm not trying to make excuses for him, but I am trying to show you how events escalated so quickly. Let's talk about the second most important point to understand about youth violence – the Violence Ladder – and maybe that'll clarify things a little.

CHRIS FELL RIGHT INTO THE GANG'S TRAP

"As I said, Stick and his friends had the whole thing figured out beforehand. They wanted to get revenge on somebody from a rival gang, and they needed a scapegoat – somebody to do the job then take the fall. And it worked. Chris is the one who went to jail, and Stick and his friends are running free. What I find frightening is the fact that Stick knew exactly how to use the Violence Ladder to his advantage. He started out by telling Chris that somebody was out to get him. That's the first step on the Violence Ladder – harassment. And Stick was ingenious about it. He blamed the harassment on somebody else and offered his friendship. Stick levered the fear he'd instilled in Chris to get him to come along for the subway ride, and he used his reputation as the cool thug to win Chris's interest. By joining Stick and the others after school, Chris took his first fatal step. He put himself in the hands of Stick's gang. He became wrapped up in the excitement, gradually losing his sense of right and wrong. Stick knew that when things got confusing, as they did when the two gangs met, Chris would be putty in his hands. The other steps on the Violence Ladder – the threats, the grouping, the weapons, and the serious violence – all happened one after the other in a few short seconds. All according to Stick's plan. It was a trap. . . ." I could see Robert shaking his head.

"Come, on, Kevin. You're making it out like Stick did the stabbing. I still say that Chris is totally responsible. Chris is his own man."

"Well," I replied, "I think that's the problem, Robert. I don't think Chris was his own man."

"Right," Wendy said. "Chris should have taken care of the problem on his own. He shouldn't have trusted those kids from the beginning. Sure, he made the wrong choice when he stabbed the other kid, but he made a wrong choice long before that. He shouldn't have gone on the subway with Stick and his friends."

"I think you're on the right track, Wendy," I said, "which leads us to the third most important point to understand about youth violence – parents can help protect their kids."

KIDS NEED TO BE INDIVIDUALS

"I think the point about being your own man – or woman for that matter – is the key, here," Lydia said. "I have three sons and I teach them to be individuals. I really impress that upon them. I know Chris didn't know what he was getting himself into, he didn't plan to hurt anybody, but he shouldn't have trusted those kids. He should have known better. I think

Chris really wanted to believe they were his friends. And I think the fact that he went with them indicates that he was sort of joining their gang."

I nodded my head. "I agree. We can't tell our kids enough that it's important to be an individual. Chris should have been wary about Stick from the beginning. If he was concerned about the rumour that someone was out to get him, he should have reported it.

SUMMARY

"Okay, I think we covered some good ground here. We've learned how subtle and sophisticated the troublemakers can be. We know how the escalation of violence can confuse kids, how it can put them in positions where they make the wrong choice. And we know that one of the best ways parents can help protect their kids is to teach them to be individuals and to think for themselves.

"Next month, I'd like to start taking an in-depth look at kids and gangs. Parents should know how gangs operate and how they victimize innocent kids. If Chris had been warned about kids like Stick, maybe he wouldn't have fallen victim to their trap, and maybe he wouldn't have crossed the line from victim to offender."

FOR KIDS VIOLENCE IS A LEGITIMATE WAY TO SOLVE PROBLEMS

I drove home slowly that night. In my mind I was going over the Chris story. I have told that story hundreds of times – not to parents, but to the kids. It's the story I use in my lecture at the schools. And I always get a mixed reaction from the kids. Some of them identify with Chris. They face the same pressures at school. They know how the tough kids use fear as a tactic. And I know a lot of them wonder what they would have done. Other kids, though, identify with Stick. They might not be instigators themselves, but they admire kids like Stick nonetheless. They think he's cool, brave. They think it's ingenious the way he got another stupid kid to do his dirty work. But the most frightening thing of all is the fact that most of the kids I speak to don't even question the act of violence itself. For them, violence is a legitimate way to solve problems. It's the only choice. It's the solution to their problems. The two rival gangs in the story sorted their differences out with violence, and nobody thought that was absurd.

It's an attitude.

4

A CHILD LOSES CONTROL

As always, I was anxious to get started and had arrived at the classroom before the November parents meeting was due to start. While I was waiting, Lydia walked up to the front of the class with her husband. "Hi, Kevin," she said. "How are you? This is my husband, Mike."

"Hi," I replied. "How are the kids?"

"They're a handful!" she said. "Greg is fifteen, Paul's ten and Joey's only nine. It's a twenty-four-hour job keeping on top of them. They're good kids, but even dealing with scrapes and bruises, making sure they get to school, get their homework done and don't disappear inside the computer all night is a wild ride. Actually, Greg and Paul have been no trouble at all, but I did want to talk to you about Joey. It was nothing like that story you told about Chris last month, that's for sure. But, well, I guess Joey just sort of took a wrong turn."

"What happened?" I asked.

TROUBLE WITH LYDIA'S SON JOEY

"Joey was only eight at the time, I guess," she said. "He was always so polite, such a good kid. Never in any trouble, good marks, just like our other two boys. But then he started hanging around with a new kid at their school, Mark. It wasn't long after that we found ourselves sitting in the vice-principal's office while he decided whether to call the police or not.

"Mark's dad had left his mom a few years earlier. Her name was Jennie, and I met her a few times. She was a nice woman. She obviously

36

cared about her two sons. But she had to work to support the three of them and she just couldn't be around enough to set them straight when things went wrong. Over time, our son Joey stopped playing with his usual friends, his personality changed, he started talking back and staying out past his curfew. We had a horrible time with him. Then one day I found a Walkman in his room. I knew it wasn't his. Anyway, by the time I had it all sorted out, after talking to Jennie and some of the other parents and the teachers, we found out that Mark and Joey had been bullying the other kids. It was extortion. They were threatening to beat up other kids in their class and making them hand over lunch money or toys or whatever. And this was in grade four!"

"Wow," I said, "I do come across those situations, even in grades as low as grade two. But you must have been very upset. What did you do?"

"Actually, Kevin," said Lydia, "I'm glad you told us that story about Chris and how he was manipulated by the other kids into joining that gang. I really empathized with him because I had seen how Joey had been influenced by a kid who was intent on making trouble. In fact, that's why I made that point at our last meeting – about stressing to your children that they have to be individuals. That's how we approached the situation with Mark and Joey. Joey was punished for what he did, everything was returned, and the school was made aware of what had been happening so that they could monitor Joey and Mark more closely. But I think the most important thing we did was to sit Joey down and really, really impress upon him how crucial it is that he think for himself. We told him not to just go along with what another kid or group of kids is telling him. He has to be able to evaluate what's going on and make his mind up about what is right and wrong. And if he's unsure about something he now knows that he should come and talk to us.

"All along he knew that taking things from other kids was wrong, we've impressed that on all our kids. But Mark, I guess, was glamourous and Joey got swept up in the excitement. He thought it was cool."

"So, how have things been since then?" I asked.

"Better than ever," smiled Mike. "Joey's marks have gone back up, he has his old friends back and we haven't been getting any nasty calls to go and see the vice-principal."

"It sounds like he was a well-grounded child to begin with," I said, "and you can take credit for that. It probably saved him from getting into more serious trouble than he did. I think you handled the situation very well. I'm impressed you were able to spot something was wrong and take action so early on."

It was seven o'clock, time to get going. I said thanks to Lydia and Mike for stopping to talk, and as they took their seats, I stood to address the room.

PAINTING A PICTURE OF YOUTH VIOLENCE

"Tonight," I said, "I'd like to start off with a story about a kid from a wealthy family who ends up forming his own gang and getting into serious trouble. This story is a good example of the Violence Ladder, and how the Violence Ladder influences gang formation. So, later in our meeting, I think we should spend some time talking about what a gang is, what they do and why kids join them.

DAVID'S STORY

"This story is fairly long and involved, but all the details will help us understand what we as parents are up against. . . . Last April, I was assigned to a case that involved a 14-year-old boy from a west-end high school. His parents were both professionals – his dad's a doctor, his mom's a lawyer. His school was not known for having a lot of violent incidents, and he had a good school record all the way up to grade eight. But, when he started grade nine, things really started to fall apart.

"His name is David and I met him when I arrested him for assault. He was just a 14-year-old kid and he was scared. But in a way he was glad he had been caught – going to jail was the end of the line and his chance to turn his life around. As I was to find in my conversations with him, he had already been up to no good for months.

"From what David told me, his problems started near the beginning of his school year. He was nervous about entering grade nine. A friend of his, Gary, had a brother in high school who had been scaring both of them with horror stories about the abuse they would get as grade nines. As you all probably remember from your own childhood, grade nine students can have it pretty rough. You go from top of the middle school to bottom of the barrel, and David was no exception. In fact, he had a run-in with a grade-ten bully right on his first day.

"As he was standing in line to pick up his schedule for the year another student banged into him from behind. David stumbled. The grade ten stranger then pushed him and screamed at him to watch where he was going. When David said he hadn't done anything, the other kid grabbed his shirt, got right in his face and hissed, 'My name's Jerry and if you know what's good for you, you'll remember that and stay the hell out of my way.'

"From what I know, Jerry had had a pretty rough year himself in grade nine, so he figured it was his turn to treat David the way he'd been treated himself the year before. And David didn't take it well at all. As I said, he was already full of anxiety and this incident only made him feel worse. Afterwards, he was careful about who he spoke to and what he said. He avoided kids he didn't know and, instead, spent all his time hanging around with his friend Gary who he thought was cool and kind of crazy. The two of them had spent a lot of time together in the previous summer, hanging out at David's parents' cottage – throwing the baseball around, swimming, and taking out the small sailboat. The two of them had known each other since grade five, and there weren't a lot of other kids from their middle school at this high school, so it was natural that they clung to each other.

"Sometime in October, Gary and David went to their first high school party. At eight o'clock on a Saturday night, Gary and David met at the subway station and began walking together to the party. Both had a palmful of gel in their slicked back hair. But Gary was wearing torn jeans, a sports jersey and was hauling a knapsack. David on the other hand looked like a complete dork, wearing corduroy pants and new silk shirt. When Gary first saw him, he burst out laughing. David felt terrible. He didn't have an older brother like Gary and he'd let his parents buy his pants. He really began to worry when Gary said, 'What were you thinking!? Girls don't like uptight guys!'

"As they walked to the party Gary tugged at David's arm and they entered a small, dimly lit park. They sat on a park bench and Gary pulled out a couple of beers from his knapsack, twisted off the caps and offered one to David. 'This should help you relax,' he said. In about fifteen minutes both of them had downed three beers. Half-loaded and ready for anything they continued to the party.

"They could hear the music blaring a few houses away. The front door was open and a bunch of teenagers were standing around on the verandah. This was the life, David figured. The days of spending Friday night on the basement couch with a bag of chips and the TV remote were behind him. He and Gary climbed the steps and nudged their way through the crowd. The partying seemed to be happening in the basement, so they pushed through the kids lining the stairs and walked down. It was nearly impossible to see or hear anything down there. The room was packed with groups of strange guys and girls talking or dancing. Some of them making out. They didn't recognize anybody and no one came over to say hi, so the two of them found an empty corner and sat on the floor. David was still a little self-conscious about how he looked.

"Most of the people there were older. It was a grade ten and eleven crowd. Gary fished through his knapsack again and pulled out a bottle of wine that he had grabbed from his Dad's cabinet. This was the first time either of them had had more than a few sips of alcohol – and they were loving it. They laughed and took heavy swigs on the bottle. They were getting quite drunk. David was eager to meet some girls and the alcohol made him feel brave enough to introduce himself – he had stopped worrying about looking like a geek.

"He stumbled to his feet, and pushed his way through the crowd. He found a spot on the floor where some girls were dancing, and started swinging his arms, bobbing his head up and down. Then he noticed that one of the girls was smiling at him. He asked her to dance. But she didn't answer. So he grabbed her hands and started dancing with her until a taller boy shoved him away. David fell back into the crowd. Ahead of him he could see someone snickering. It was Jerry. At school he had gone out of his way to avoid running into Jerry, turning and walking the long way around to his get to his classes whenever he saw him. Jerry poked his finger in David's chest, looked him in the eye and said, 'Leave now.'

"Quickly, David found Gary in the corner and suggested they leave. Out on the street, they ran into a couple of other new grade nines, Darren and Ian, who had given up on the party as well. The four of them walked back to the park and sat there, smoking cigarettes and finishing off the last of Gary's wine. Gary was upset about leaving and wanted to take some revenge. The grade tens at the party had totally ignored him, even the ones who were friends of his brothers – the ones who used to come over to swim in the pool at his parents house. Even his own brother had turned and walked the other way when he saw Gary sitting in the corner. Everyone thought they were too cool to say hi to a grade nine and it made Gary burn. But he had a plan.

"After a brief discussion, the four kids walked back toward the house. Five cars were parked in the driveway, and others lined the curb along the street. Gary looked toward the front porch. The door was open slightly, but nobody stood on the verandah. He gave the signal and the four kids split up, each walking quietly down the sides of the different cars. A moment later they regrouped on the sidewalk and made their way quickly and quietly back to the park. They waited until they were four blocks away before laughing their heads off. They had just keyed six cars, scraped the paint off their side doors in neat grooves. David had never done anything like it before – but it felt great. The guilt that nagged at him was drowned out, not just by the alcohol, but by the high of getting away scot-free.

"The four of them hung around the park for a while laughing and talking about what they had done. But soon the temperature started to drop and the booze began to wear off. David decided it was time to go home.

"Even though David was exhausted – from the booze and the excitement – he told me he didn't sleep well that night. He kept waking up, hot and sweaty. The guilt had gotten to him, he said.

"In class on Monday morning an announcement was made about the party in the neighbourhood and the keying incident. The car owners were asking for witnesses to the event. When David heard this his heart jolted. He glanced around and saw Ian, in the row ahead, turn and wink. David stifled a nervous giggle. They had shared an experience that glued them together. Secretly, he worried that someone had seen them. But days went by and nothing more was said about the incident. Eventually, David stopped thinking about it.

"The four kids started spending their Friday nights together, meeting after school and going downtown to blow twenty bucks each on video games in the arcades. Occasionally they'd go see a movie, but most of the time they would just hang out in the local stores or on the street corners talking to other kids. Some nights all they did was walk around downtown. They couldn't find anything to do. Boredom was setting in, but it didn't take long before they found some excitement.

"One Friday night, while the four of them were browsing through a record store, David found a CD he'd been looking for. He went to the counter to pay for it, but Ian tugged at his arm and told him not to be stupid – 'only idiots pay cash for their CDs.' David didn't understand what Ian meant until Ian grabbed the CD from David and walked right out of the store. The four of them met around the corner, and Ian handed David the CD. He told him it was a gift. David excitedly shoved the CD into his jacket.

"Eventually, shoplifting CDs became a regular Friday night activity. The kids were even competitive about it, seeing who could steal the most CDs in one go. Ian was the champ with five CDs. At first, David was nervous at the thought of shoplifting. What if he got caught? On a few occasions, he'd gone into the record store with the intention of stealing but came out empty-handed. His friends called him a wimp. He couldn't stand the ribbing, so he promised himself he wouldn't chicken out next time. So, one night, he spent over half an hour pouring through the CD racks before managing to slip one into his jacket pocket. He told me his hands were trembling as he walked through the doorway, trying his best not to look suspicious. Outside, he tore down the street and met up with his friends. They exchanged pats on the back and slapped hands. David's heart was racing, the thrill he'd gotten after keying those cars was back. It was great. Eventually David managed to snag three CDs in one haul – close to Ian's record of five.

"Stealing was exciting. At last, the four kids – David, Gary, Ian and Darren – had found a way out of their bored lives. They were now a tight brotherhood, and the brotherhood was about to get deeper into trouble.

"From hanging out on the downtown streets, the four kids started mixing with street people. They met runaway girls who'd become hookers, homeless young people who slept in alleys or on grates, and teenage drug dealers hustling them to buy anything from marijuana to coke or even crack. None of the group had ever done drugs – David hadn't even really thought about it. After all, he'd only had his first beer a few weeks ago. He was still unsure about doing something so illegal, and – more than anything – he was worried about what pot or hash would do to him. His parents had told him drugs were dangerous and the TV was always carrying messages about the evils of drug addiction and the penalties for getting caught. But out on the streets everyone seemed to be doing it. It was cool and somebody was always trying to convince them they'd enjoy it – that it would change their lives. Then, one night, as they stood on a street corner trying to think of something to do, they were approached by a dealer who was desperate to unload his marijuana, whatever the price. They purchased a couple of joints that were already rolled, ducked into an alley behind a Chinese restaurant and lit one up. David said he was surprised at how mild the effects were. It made him feel a little groggy – but nicely relaxed and happy as well. The four of them agreed they enjoyed it – a lot.

"They started buying pot regularly. Drugs and shoplifting became their twin pastimes on Friday night. At first, they kept their drug taking to the streets, but after a few weeks, David and Gary started bringing drugs to school, occasionally smoking up between classes. Sometimes, the dope made them too lethargic to go to their afternoon classes. David said it was much easier to simply ditch the afternoon and veg in the park. He had never skipped classes before, because in their middle school teachers wouldn't let them get away with stuff like that, but in high school they were on their own more. Students were supposed to need less supervision, and David started enjoying his new freedom. Soon they were missing several classes a week. They stopped doing their homework altogether. By Christmas, with exams fast approaching, David realized he'd hardly read any of his school books. He knew his grades were going in the toilet. But all he wanted to do was escape. His drug use, delinquency and absenteeism simply got worse. Needless to say, he did terribly on his exams.

"Gary had never been a top student, so his marks, although bad, were not much different than the results he got in middle school. But David's overall marks had dropped fifteen percent. His first semester average was sixty, compared to seventy-five in grade eight.

"One afternoon, during the Christmas break, David came home and as he was going up the stairs he heard his father calling for him. His report card had arrived in the mail. David hadn't spoken much to his dad in the past few months – he was usually out with his friends or on the phone by the time his dad came home from the office. So, when he walked into his dad's study he felt a little nervous. His dad was eager to know why his marks had dropped so drastically. David fumbled with his words at first, but managed to explain how high school was so much harder than middle school. He admitted he was having some trouble adjusting to the pace, the new schedule and the different people, but promised to work harder.

That seemed to suffice. His dad dismissed him, and David went upstairs, mumbling to himself about what an annoying jerk his dad was. Why the hell should his dad care what kind of marks he got. It was none of his business. Up in his room, David sneaked a cigarette and smoked his nerves and anger away.

"Drugs weren't the reason David and I met. In fact, I found out about David's drug problem later during my investigation into assault charges that were laid against him.

"The incident that led to the charges took place in February, at a local party that David and his friends had crashed. They weren't the most popular kids in school, not by a mile. And they definitely hadn't been invited to this event. A girl was throwing a party while her parents were out of town and tons of kids had shown up. Hundreds of them packed the rooms in the house, even the bedrooms on the third floor. David, Gary, Ian and Darren had been walking along a nearby street when they heard the noise coming from the party. They were giddy from smoking a joint a little earlier and thought it would be fun to just walk in on this party. They entered the front door and stepped into the kitchen, then, taking advantage of their anonymity they raided the fridge for beer. They found a corner in the living room and huddled there, drinking. Nobody asked who they were, and they sat there for more than an hour, drinking and laughing. They all got pretty buzzed. At about 11 o'clock someone in the crowd spotted them – it was Jerry.

"Jerry marched over to their corner. Staring hard at the four of them he told them to get the hell out. But David, high from the pot and the beers, just laughed and told him to buzz off. Jerry glared at him, then picked him up by the collar, screaming into his face, calling him every insulting thing he could think of, and then threw him back a few feet. By now, a crowd had gathered round. David, feeling brave, cocked his fist to take a punch. Jerry saw what was coming, grabbed David's arms and kneed him in the groin. David stumbled back, coughing. Jerry stood over him as he caught his breath and then shoved him out of the house.

"Gary, Ian and Darren quickly followed behind David. Outside, they started fuming and swearing. They wanted to get even again. But this time they weren't just going to key a few cars. They were bolder now, more confident after their experiences in the last few months. They came up with a plan.

"The four of them walked up the front steps, but by now it was locked. So they sneaked around to the back of the house, where they found a group of kids huddled in a circle, passing a joint around. The glass sliding doors to the basement were open, so David and his friends walked inside, then made their way through the hallway and up the stairs. At the main floor landing, Ian and Darren carefully scanned the area. They spotted Jerry talking to a girl by the front door lobby. They called out his name, waited till Jerry noticed them, and then hurried back downstairs.

"Jerry ran after them, but as he was running down the basement stairs he tripped and flew forward, crashing on the carpeted floor. He scrambled to his feet, saw David and lunged forward, grabbing him by the neck. David elbowed Jerry in the stomach, and Jerry followed with a punch to the head. But, by now, Jerry was surrounded by David's friends – they dove on him and started throwing wild punches. The pot smokers came inside to watch, and a crowd of other people rushed down from upstairs. Jerry managed to swing around and connect with a solid punch into Gary's face. David, enraged and in a frenzy, grabbed for a nearby hockey stick, swung it high, and smashed it down over Jerry's head. Jerry collapsed onto the floor. He was bleeding badly from a head wound. David just stood there, stunned at what he'd done.

"One of the witnesses called emergency and I showed up a few minutes later. An ambulance arrived shortly after I did and took Jerry to the hospital. I charged David and his friends with assault, and took them into custody. At the hospital Jerry received forty stitches, but didn't suffer any permanent damage."

I saw Robert put up his hand. "Kevin," he said, "you spoke to David after he'd been arrested. What did he think about the whole thing?"

"Well," I began, "on the night of the assault, I interviewed David at the station. I sat him down on a wooden chair in the middle of one of the interview rooms, and asked to hear his side of the story. Our session lasted nearly an hour, and David talked very openly the whole time, apologizing to me for what he'd done. He sobbed uncontrollably. I felt sorry for him. Obviously, he had never expected to end up at a police station. He was still in shock, I think – not believing what he'd done. In fact, most of the kids I arrest end up breaking down like that. It's not unusual for them to bawl and shake wildly – which is such a startling contrast to the violent behaviour that led to their arrest. I can only imagine how they feel. When they are caught their entire sense of power and control vanishes. One minute they are riding high and feeling powerful, the next minute they're cringing in the corner of a police station. It's definitely a rude awakening.

"What is curious about many of these kids is the relief they seem to experience after getting caught, as though, secretly, that's what they wanted. For many of them, the gang life is a downward spiral, and they don't know how to jump off it. So they keep going and going until we catch them, and that's the only way they get free. For David, a west-end high-school boy from a well-to-do family, spending five days in jail was the height of shame. But I got the sense that he was glad it was all over. . . ."

5

ALL ABOUT GANGS

I sat down at the teacher's desk while everyone got up to stretch their legs and refill their coffee cups. I could hear parents talking about David's story, and there was definite concern in their voices. Parents from good neighbourhoods often see youth violence as someone else's problem. Now they're probably wondering if their children have friends like David. I was encouraged because David's story was such an eye-opener.

"Okay," I said, "as promised at the beginning of this meeting, I'd like to discuss David's story as an example of the Violence Ladder and gang formation, but before we do that we're going to take a closer look at gangs. There are 3 major questions about gangs that I think we need to answer. First – what is a gang? Second – what do gangs do? And, third – why do kids join gangs? This will take a while but it is very important.

QUESTION 1: WHAT IS A GANG?

"Probably the best definition I can give you of a gang is one developed by Dr. Fred Mathews. According to Dr. Mathews, a gang or, what we've also been calling a group, is made up of three or more youths. Membership in this group can be a fluid thing, but there is always a stable core of members who think of themselves as a gang or a group. Sometimes they might just be a group of kids hanging out together. They may stick together for social, cultural, or other reasons. But we see them as a gang because they either spontaneously commit, or plan to commit, anti-social, delinquent or illegal acts. In a nutshell that's the definition of a gang. So you see, it's very broad. And you don't need dozens of kids to make a gang. All you need is three."

THE STEREOTYPE

Robert, who had been shaking his head while I was talking, suddenly spoke up, "Kevin, I'm not sure I'm buying all this gang stuff. I mean, you tell us these stories and you have these figures, but I just don't see it. You know, I pick my sons up here after school every night and I don't see any gangs."

"What does a gang look like?" I asked him.

"I don't know. . . . Like they do in the movies?" he said.

"I guess you're talking about movies like *Colors* and *Boyz 'N' the Hood*. Kids with nylon track suits and unlaced basketball shoes," I replied. "Yeah, you're right, some gangs look like that. But only the hard-core street gangs. And I think kids pick up lots about the L.A. gangs from those Hollywood movies and then imitate it at their own schools. They want to be like the Crips and the Bloods, the really nasty gangs in L.A. Those are their heroes. They worship them. They think those guys are tough and powerful. They start dressing like them, adopting the same mannerisms and symbols. For instance, the Latino gangs in L.A. wear a typical uniform of baggy blue jeans, high-top running shoes, backwards baseball cap. And we're seeing the same uniform with the Latino kids in Toronto. Granted, these are the really bad gangs, and what I'm talking about in most of our local schools here is not really connected to them, but the bad gangs are spreading too. The really organized gangs are making inroads into our schools. It's like marketing. If you're selling tractors you go to the farms and talk to the farmers, you put ads in farming magazines. If you're a gang, you go to where the kids are, and that's the schools.

"Overall though, I think the stereotype of the hard-core gang is misleading. The problems we are having today – in the schools and on the streets – are not caused just by the hard-core gangs. In fact, the majority of the crimes are not. We're seeing kids from all sorts of backgrounds in groups and gangs. One of the most widely spread misconceptions these days is that only poor kids, or kids from bad neighbourhoods, get in trouble. But, as we've seen in the stories we've discussed, the gang problem is really made up of kids from all sorts of backgrounds. And the number of kids involved in gangs from middle-class and even upper-class families is alarming.

"The hard-core gangs might be the most vicious and violent, but youth crime and violence is committed by a whole spectrum of gang and group types. At one end you have the hard-core gangs and at the other end you have these loose groups of friends – like David and his buddies. And in between we see different levels of commitment–"

Robert cut in, "But a group of kids is a just a group of kids. How can you link them together with the East L.A. gangs?"

"What I'm saying is we are seeing groups of friends responsible for a lot of mischief and crime. Sure, sometimes a group of friends is just a group of friends, and no one is worrying about that. But sometimes these groups of friends cross the line and start stealing, damaging property, or assaulting other kids. When they do that, we call them a gang. And, that's what Fred Mathews's definition is saying.

"I want to impress upon you how complex the whole phenomenon is. There are no simple answers to the questions we are going to talk about tonight. As we just mentioned, gangs come in all shapes and sizes. Some are small, some large, and usually the small gangs are terrified of the bigger ones. Some gangs are highly organized, some loosely organized. Some gangs last for years, some for a moment. Some wear a type of uniform and have names. Some don't. Sometimes gang members carry knives, sometimes they carry guns. Sometimes they steal, sometimes they kill –"

MISCONCEPTIONS AND THE STEREOTYPE

Lydia spoke up, "When I hear stuff like this I just want to pack my bags and move to some hideaway in the country."

There were rumblings in the room. I guess Lydia's sentiment had struck a few sympathetic cords. I repositioned myself on the desktop. "Well, I'm certainly not here to scare anybody. I simply want you to know the truth. Before each of you started coming to our regular monthly meetings, I'm sure you had your own ideas of what the problems are with youth gangs. And these were probably largely based on what you've read in the papers, or have seen on TV. In fact, I bet some of you have seen a TV movie called *Little Criminals* where this kid goes around burning buildings and then shoots and kills someone." I saw a bunch of heads nod. "Well, I know that kids like that exist. But it seems that these more violent or sensational stories are the only ones that parents hear about.

The difficulty I see with this is that no one is paying attention to the other types of problems – the low-level stuff, the petty thefts, the intimidation, the bullying, the fear. Certainly the cost for the violent crimes is huge. I'm not downplaying that at all, but I think the cost for the other stuff is high as well. Take a look at schools – the psychological damage from fear and intimidation ruins the learning environment. That's serious stuff. So, if we don't see visible signs of damage, like property destroyed or someone injured, that doesn't mean there's not a problem. . . . I want to give you as accurate a picture of the situation as possible. The youth problems that confront us range from the heinous acts of the hard-core gangs all the way to the subtle tactics of a small group of school kids."

GROUPS

"Okay, I'd like to say something here," said Wendy, cutting in. "I guess some parents feel like Robert does, but I know I don't. I am extremely worried about the gang problem, and I know other parents who are too. I guess you're saying we should be concerned about the more informal gangs. Maybe you could tell us more about them – how they form, what they're capable of."

"Informal gangs are the most common, so you're right to be concerned," I said. "They usually form wherever kids meet each other – at school, at a mall, a community centre, or in the neighbourhood where they live. The kids start hanging out together, and wherever you get kids you're bound to get some kind of mischief. But, sometimes the mischief gets out of hand."

"What do you mean 'gets out of hand'? Do you mean they don't intend to do what they do?" Wendy asked.

"Sometimes they plan their actions, and sometimes it just erupts spontaneously. Shoplifting, for example, is often the kind of thing they will plan to do. They'll pick a store, scope it out for cops, and if the coast is clear, they'll go in and raid the place. But other things they do, like vandalism or swarming, just happen. Which is frightening, because there's no way to tell when it's coming, and the factors involved in making it happen are a little mysterious. With swarming, escalation up the Violence Ladder happens in a matter of seconds – so there's no time to break it."

COLOURS, GANG NAMES AND STREET NAMES

"I know you said it's difficult to tell if a gang is a gang. But are there clues? You know, do most gangs wear similar clothing and that kind of thing?" Mary asked.

"Some groups do wear similar colours – we think of them as uniforms – but a lot don't. If they do wear uniforms it might be just that they all wear the same colour, or the same baseball hat, or the same type of jacket, maybe the same sports team jacket."

"Do they have names?" Mary asked.

"Most of these groups don't have names, but some do. And the ones that do will sometimes use the name of a popular gang from the States, like the Bloods or the Crips. They're copycat gangs. They'll try and mimic the gangs they see in movies and music videos. This 'gangsta' culture glorifies violence. For them these U.S. gangs are cool.

"In Toronto alone there are over 160 gangs. A significant number of them are highly organized, which is frightening. But, as I've said, the majority of these gangs are less organized. They might have a leader, but it will usually be whoever is the most popular kid at the time. And popularity is a fickle thing, so the 'leader' changes depending on which way the wind is blowing."

"Do the kids themselves have nicknames?" Mary asked.

"Yes," I said, "but we don't call them nicknames. We call them street names. An example of a street name is Stick, who was the gang member in Chris's story, the one who gave Chris the knife and told him to stab the rival gang member."

"Why do they use these street names?"

"To protect their identity. If we don't know their real name, it's hard for us to track them down. A street name makes them sound cool.

QUESTION 2: WHAT DO GANGS DO?

I noticed Wendy's hand go up so I motioned in her direction.

"Okay," she said, "I think I've got a good picture of what a gang is. What I'm curious about now is the damage that these gangs are doing. I mean, we seem to be focusing on the groups that are less extreme, not the ones running drugs or shooting each other, but the less organized groups of kids in our own schools. What are the most harmful things that these groups do?"

THE FOUR TYPES OF GANG BEHAVIOUR

"To me," I said, "the four types of gang behaviour are: vandalism and tagging; harassment; extortion; and violence. I think we should spend a few minutes discussing each.

BEHAVIOUR 1: VANDALISM AND TAGGING

"I'm sure we've all seen spray-painted slogans and signs scrawled across the sides of buildings in various parts of the city. In some places the graffiti is so thick that you can no longer see the wall beneath it. Sprayed pictures or words are what the gangs call 'tags' – visual signals that the gangs use to mark their territory. Typically a gang will cover every possible surface in their neighbourhood – their turf – with their tag. This announces to other gangs or groups that they are trespassing and should be ready to deal with the consequences – which may be harassment or violence.

"Many people see these markings everyday but don't really notice them. Often boys will even put a tag in one of their girlfriend's school books. Parents sometimes see them, but think they are just doodles. Unfortunately, graffiti has become a part of the urban fabric – just another aspect of living in a city. Even the owners of the buildings where the tagging is done often don't do anything about it. They don't even try to clean it off, which can actually be quite dangerous.

"All of us have seen groups of young kids hanging around in the food court area after school and thought nothing of it. And sometimes, maybe there is nothing to it. Maybe they're just bored or killing time. But sometimes separate cliques start to develop. One kid might have an argument with another kid and their two peer groups suddenly drift apart – each kid sticking up for his friend. The food court now becomes the object of a small turf war. And in order to establish territory, one group will usually lay claim to what they consider their space by tagging the walls. I'm sure some of you have noticed designs, letters or slogans painted or scratched on the pillars or walls or in the bathrooms of your local mall. If those tags aren't removed promptly by the mall management, the kids from the other group will read it and see it as a challenge. And, if they in turn spray-paint over the tags, the original group will have to get their revenge. It's another example of the Violence Ladder, because each act from then on is going to increase the likelihood of violence, and if the Violence Ladder isn't broken, someone will get hurt.

"This kind of tagging takes place everyday in schools and neighbourhoods across the country. If a group has their tags on a certain area they feel they own that place. In their eyes, it's their property. But these tags go further than just establishing turf. They also help give the group a sense of identity. Individual kids will start to feel a deep attachment to the group, and they'll become more aggressive and daring about protecting the group as a whole. Because tagging is so pervasive, few kids ever consider that it is actually against the law. But it is vandalism and it is illegal, and that alone makes a group that happens to spray-paint a wall a gang in the eyes of the law.

BEHAVIOUR 2: HARASSMENT

"Another significant gang behaviour is harassment, which is one of the most common problems in our schools. As I mentioned in our first meeting, when I say harassment I mean low-level harassment such as when one kid calls another kid an idiot, or gives him the finger, or bumps into him in the hall. And don't forget, it's also the first step on the Violence Ladder. Harassment is one of the first things that kids who have formed groups or gangs at school start doing. For them it's a way of asserting power and gaining recognition. Next month's story deals with stalking, a typical example of harassment. Stalking is when kids follow right behind another kid as he or she walks from class to class. They move in total silence, not saying a word. It's terrifying for the victim—"

"That's awful," Mary exclaimed. "It ruins the whole learning atmosphere."

"Yes. Exactly. I think that's the worst thing about it. It creates a terrible atmosphere for learning. School is hard enough for a lot of kids, but to be dealing with fear all the time, that's dreadful. The learning environment is poisoned. If a student is afraid, how can they learn? Imagine going to work and worrying constantly whether the other employees were going to beat you up in the washroom."

"These schools are so different and strange compared to the adult world we live in," Wendy added from her seat at the back. "It's really hard for me to totally comprehend, but, yeah, it would be like me looking over my shoulder all the time at the office, scared to leave my desk for lunch."

Behaviour 3: Extortion

"Yes," I agreed, "you can imagine how it feels. Though there's no real physical harm, the psychological damage is very serious. Let's turn now to extortion, which is also common in the schools. Extortion is when someone uses threats, accusation or violence to obtain something – like money, a jacket or a Walkman – from another person. If you remember, we came across a form of extortion in our first story. In that case Rick was trying to weasel twenty bucks out of Jamie, telling him he had to buy a knife. Of course, the knife was only a ruse, and Rick was planning to just take the twenty dollars and run. There are literally thousands of kids like Jamie in schools all across our country who, on a regular basis, are asked by kids in gangs to cough up money for various reasons. They're handing over their lunch money and going hungry and their parents don't know about it.

"A few months ago I was called in on a case that happened at a nearby school. The kids that went there were from well-off families. They wore expensive jackets, high-end running shoes, and because of this they were the target of a gang that had come in all the way from the suburbs. Every lunch hour, the gang would walk around on the school property and tell the students that if they didn't hand over their lunch money somebody would get them. This went on for weeks – nearly every lunch hour – until finally one of the victims told the principal and we managed to arrest the offenders. When we asked them why they had come all the way from outside the city, they told us they had nothing better to do and figured they could get some money and cool clothes from these rich kids.

"I find the attitude towards extortion amongst gang kids frightening. They just see something they want, like someone's Walkman or jacket, and they take it. Zero compunction. No guilt about what they are doing to the other kid. No worries at all about the consequences of their actions. They're certainly not afraid of the Young Offenders Act. They're not thinking about a potential jail term. I'm not sure that many of them even realize that they're committing a serious crime.

"It's just so easy for them to take what they want – three or four kids will just walk up to another kid and grab for the item. If there's any resistance, the kid gets hit, and that's that. The gang walks away with a Walkman or jacket, or whatever – leaving the poor victim beaten, robbed and humiliated. In fact, that humiliation is a key to this type of gang behaviour. It's more than just wanting the kid's Walkman. And in some cases it's obviously not about the Walkman. Once again, it's all about power for the kids who are in gangs. We're beginning to believe that the major motivation in most cases isn't the Walkman or greed in general, but the power and thrill of humiliating another human being.

BEHAVIOUR 4: VIOLENCE

"The final type of gang behaviour is violence. Unlike harassment or extortion, where the damage may be only psychological, the damage from violence is both psychological and physical – and may leave long-lasting scars. In the extreme, it may even mean a life is lost. In fact, a 1994 study done by the Canadian Research Institute for Law and the Family on behalf of the Calgary Police Service concluded that violence was a serious concern for many students in our country's schools. The survey showed that over half of the students were worried that they would get threatened or hurt at school. And just under half of them were worried that someone would punch or kick them, or that a gang would beat them up.

"By examining the Violence Ladder over the past few months, we have seen how relatively insignificant acts like harassment and threats can lead to violence. But once the violence starts, it escalates – from kicks and punches to serious woundings and, in the most nightmarish cases, to killings.

"For example, if a bunch of kids have resorted to punching another kid – say, punching him in the shoulder as he walks down the hall – the victim may gather his friends around and return the physical abuse later in the day. The next day, one of the groups is likely to take it to the next level, and the beatings get worse. One of them will eventually pull out a bat or a knife. And after that, a gun may enter the picture. That's how the violence escalates. It's an arms race. And that's why it's so crucial to break the Violence Ladder as early as possible."

SOME TEACHERS ARE AFRAID

"Can't the teachers do anything?" asked Mary.

"Well, in many cases they do," I replied, "but they aren't always around to prevent gang behaviour. It doesn't always happen in the classroom or even on school property. Plus, the teachers themselves are not immune to harassment or violence. Remember, things have changed since we were in school. Nowadays teachers feel they can't discipline children or speak loudly to them because they might find themselves in court justifying themselves criminally or civilly."

"So you mean even the teachers are afraid of these kids?" she asked.

"Sure. And, to tell the truth, they have good reason to be. I think that not going to the school board or calling us is the wrong thing to do, but I totally understand their fear. I'm not saying they shouldn't be concerned, but they aren't doing themselves any good when they let the kids know they're afraid. One teacher I know paid the price for not going for help.

"Some kids started acting up in his class, talking while he was trying to teach. He told them to be quiet but they wouldn't stop. They started swearing at him, threatening him, and this went on for the next fifteen minutes till the class ended. After the bell rang, one of the troublemakers approached the teacher and told him if he reported anything, he'd be sorry. So he didn't. Then for the rest of the year, the class was a complete nightmare. All the students suffered, and none of the other kids said anything, because they were scared too. They thought, well, if the teacher isn't doing anything about it, then I'm not going to risk anything either.

"When problems aren't reported the Violence Ladder is allowed to continue and the behaviour escalates. This is just as true for teachers and school staff as it is for kids. When threats and harassment aren't reported and dealt with immediately, it means that we completely lose control of the situation and violence becomes a real possibility.

DRUGS AND RACE

"Briefly, I'd like to mention two of the most common things that people associate with gangs – drugs and racial violence. Drugs and racial violence are certainly related to youth gangs and in some cases they are deeply entwined in the gang phenomenon. However, this is only true in certain neighbourhoods, and the two problems are not as widespread as most people believe. Let's take a look at the reality.

DRUGS

"A few years ago, there really wasn't much of a connection between youth gangs and drugs. But this seems to be changing. Drugs are finding their way into the youth gang problem because drug pushers see schools as a way of gaining new customers. They infiltrate the school grounds and look for kids to sell drugs to. And once the kids get hooked, they have to steal money to buy the drugs. Joining a gang or forming a gang is the easiest way for them to get quick money. Sometimes the gangs will get involved in the drug trade as a way of paying for their habit or making a profit. And, as you can imagine, where drugs are involved we often find weapons and violence.

"However, the point I want to make is that we find lots of violence and weapons use in the schools where no drugs are involved at all. So, in some cases, drugs are part of the problem. They certainly make things worse, but many gangs exist without drugs.

RACE

"As far as racial violence goes, there really isn't much of a connection with the informal type of gangs we've been talking about. These loose groups of friends are a real mixed bag. Membership is very lax – whoever is hanging out at the mall, or the school playground can become a member. But there are gangs that do organize along ethnic and cultural lines. And the truth is we are seeing more of these formal gangs nowadays.

"Conflicts between racially or culturally different groups often start with small incidents at school. A few weeks ago there was a massive fight at a suburban high school. It started because an Asian student didn't like the way a black student looked at him. They each gathered their friends, which tended to be of the same ethnicity, and a fight broke out. In this case it didn't really start out as a race issue, but it developed into one because ultimately it was a group of Asians against a group of blacks, but it could be any race or culture.

"Sometimes the issues are more obviously racial, or cultural. We see kids of the same cultural background hanging out together because they share so much in common – the same values, similar dress and musical tastes. This common ground serves to give these kids a sense of belonging. And sometimes they feel the need to assert their differences. We've seen fights break out because one kid insults another kid's accent. And nowadays we are beginning to see really narrow definitions of ethnicity – kids not just with the same skin colour, but kids with families that come from the same country. So you might have two black gangs warring against each other, one from the Caribbean and one from Africa."

"What about gangs like neo-nazis, skinheads, that type of thing? That stuff really terrifies me," Jackie said.

"Yes. We do have gangs like that. And they are a very serious concern. The media has paid a lot of attention to them because their activities are sensational, but in terms of numbers, they are a very small part of the problem. The media has also popularized other sensational gang types — like the kind that riots after a rock concert, where kids spill out into the street together and assault people or damage property. But again, though this activity is heinous, it is only a fraction of the problem, and the kids doing this kind of thing are largely strangers to each other.

QUESTION 3: WHY DO KIDS JOIN GANGS?

"Okay," I said, "I'd like to switch gears now and move on to a slightly different aspect of the gang phenomenon. If gangs are so destructive why is it that so many kids, even surprisingly good kids, want to join? We see kids of all ages involved in gangs, from kids in grade one who gang up on other students in the playground to twenty-one-year-olds who swarm strangers on the streets. They come from all backgrounds and areas of the country. What many parents ask me when confronted with these facts is, 'Kevin, don't they realize they're getting themselves in trouble?'

"That's probably the most important question in this whole issue, and one that demands an open mind. I think it's very important to try to look at it from the kid's perspective. From our point of view, joining a gang is a very foolish thing, but that's not how the kids see it. It might be hard for us adults to accept it, but these kids get a lot out of being in a gang. In a warped way, there are lots of benefits to being in a gang. And this is a key point. Kids don't join a gang because they want to get into trouble, they join a gang because it's the easiest solution to their problems. Put simply, gangs meet many of the needs of these young kids."

"What kind of problems could gangs possibly solve for these kids?" Mary asked.

ACCEPTANCE

"There are lots of reasons kids form gangs. Remember how tough it was when you went to school. Remember how you wanted so badly for people to like you. Well, it's the same nowadays, except that the major way to feel like you're accepted is to join a gang. It's the quickest route. You have instant friends. That's hard to beat for a lot of kids. It's tough just being yourself and finding friends the hard way. Myself, I remember being lonely a lot of the time at school, but eventually I got to know some of the other kids, and we'd hang out together after school, playing basketball, or just running to the corner store for chocolate bars. But, it took months to build up those friendships. Today, if I was in school and needed friends badly, I could have fifteen real close friends by the end of the day, if I joined a gang.

POPULARITY

"Some kids, though, want more than just acceptance. They want everyone to know who they are. And, instead of becoming the star football player, or the top student, kids are turning to gangs to gain popularity. You know, if you're the top student, some kids will respect you, but most will hate you. If you're the football star, a lot of kids just won't care. But if you're the most feared kid in the entire school, everyone's paying attention. And, of course, being the football star or the top student just isn't a believable option for many of these kids. They might think they're not smart enough or not fast enough, but anyone can carry a gun.

"Joining a gang is the fast track to popularity. For a shy kid who's having trouble meeting new friends, being lonely is a very serious problem. It's ruining his life. He sees how many friends a gang kid has and how much attention the gang kid is getting from the other students, and he knows he can have that kind of status tomorrow if he joins. Nothing really comes close to gangs as a way of attaining popularity.

PROTECTION

"Of course, another major reason for joining a gang, or forming a gang is for protection. Many kids feel that the school system won't protect them from getting hurt, so they take care of themselves, and the resources they turn to are friends and weapons. This becomes more common when kids get dismissed or ignored. A kid will go to his home-room teacher or the principal or even to his parents and tell them that he's been threatened, and the adult will tell him not to worry about it or tell him it's no big deal. When this happens the kids just stop going to adults for help. They figure their need for protection and safety is best met by forming a gang. Violence is the solution of choice. They can't think of other alternatives. So if they feel threatened, that's what they'll turn to. I've seen this a lot. Revenge is, in fact, a major reason for gathering a gang together. When someone gets punched or has something stolen, chances are he'll gather his friends together to take on the perpetrators instead of reporting it.

A SENSE OF FAMILY

"Kids also join gangs because it gives them a sense of family. I see this a lot with kids who, like David from tonight's story, come from families where the parents are really busy and don't have time for their kids. It is also especially true of kids who have single parents who, with busy work schedules, are incredibly strapped for time. Gangs give kids the attention they don't get at home. Kids who join gangs turn to the other gang members for guidance, support and understanding instead of turning to their parents. Many of them feel so close to their group of friends that, in fact, they start calling it a family. This is a big problem among latchkey kids. However, all children who lack a sense of belonging will find the necessary community in a gang.

ENTERTAINMENT

"Kids also have a need for entertainment and excitement, and gang activities meet this need as well. It's real life entertainment for them. They get a thrill out of the various gang behaviours – the vandalism, the harassment, the extortion and violence. And of course, all the violence on TV and in music doesn't help. It makes them think of violence as an acceptable means of solving problems and as an acceptable means of entertainment. They lose perspective. Some of these kids are addicted to the thrill of getting away with a crime. That's their high, their drug. Bored kids are particularly susceptible to this thrilling aspect of gang culture.

IDENTITY AND SELF-ESTEEM

"Another thing to keep in mind is the fact that all adolescents struggle with their sense of identity. At some point all kids need to break away from their parents and develop their own identity. I know for me this happened when I turned thirteen. The next couple of years were strange and difficult, and puberty certainly mixed things up a little. Kids at this age are extremely vulnerable to bad influences. They are searching for something that gives them a sense of identity, a sense of self-esteem, and some way to express their new-found sexuality. Gangs are the instant answer. In a gang, kids can create an identity by playing around with roles. A boy might try and be the tough guy, the bully, the daring guy, the kid who will try anything – accomplishments like stealing from some kid's locker, or ripping off a store are respected and admired. His peers congratulate him and tell him he's great. It gives him a sense of pride. So gangs are a superb way of showing that you're a man, that you're brave and tough. And as far as exploring sexual identity goes, gangs are a social network, a way of meeting girls.

POWER AND CONTROL

"Kids that feel powerless in their lives also tend to turn to gangs as a way of expressing power. Ganging up on other kids, stealing something, evading the law – these things make the kids feel they have power and control in their life.

MATERIAL NEEDS

"In some cases gangs simply meet a kid's material needs. Kids that need to have the latest running shoes, the most expensive jackets, state-of-the-art Walkmans – sometimes these kids turn to gangs as a way of gaining those possessions. They can steal what they want or they can earn the money to buy stuff by trafficking drugs."

THINGS HAVE CHANGED

"But we all had these needs when we were young. How come we weren't running off with gangs?" Robert asked.

"Good question, and one I've thought a lot about. My guess is that hundreds of factors are involved. Today's world is so different than the one you or I grew up in. I know that the lack of jobs has something to do with it. When we were young, there was lots of opportunity, and we had a bright future to look forward to. Nowadays, kids don't have confidence in the future. The anxiety in the media about the economy and prospects for employment affects the attitude of these kids. I also know that kids don't have the respect for adults that we used to have. When I was young I remember having respect for the police, for my teachers, for the politicians that ran the country – they were all real people. But today, so many public figures are wrapped in scandal that our children really don't respect or trust anybody. And of course, I would say music, television and movies all contribute to the problem – they give the kids heroes that are not real. It's obvious that the media influences our children, and there is no doubt it contributes to violence. Certainly there are people who can go to a violent movie and come out of it not wanting to hurt or kill people, but that's not true of everybody. Especially not kids who are impressionable. Also, kids are seeing much more violent stuff than we ever did. I don't think I personally saw anything very violent on TV or in a movie until I was a teenager and watched *A Clockwork Orange*. Now, kids routinely see violence glorified, and that's the message they come away with. Violence is cool. And violence is the way to solve problems. The fictional characters played by Van Damme and Schwarzenegger are their heroes.

"The family environment is probably the most important factor. If the home environment is hostile, the kids are encouraged to seek comfort elsewhere. Another problem is, if the parents aren't strict enough, the kids will try to get away with as much as they can. We know the lack of limits and boundaries has a lot to do with kids getting into trouble. The reverse is true as well. If there are too many rules at home, the environment may be too stifling, and the kid just has to find a way to break loose. The freedom of being in a gang is a great solution for them."

CONSEQUENCES

Robert asked, "I'm not quite sure I understand what's going on in the heads of these kids. You've talked about all the benefits they get from being in a gang, but what about the costs? These kids are getting into serious trouble.

Some of them are breaking the law. I think going to jail is a cost that far outweighs the benefits of acceptance or popularity or entertainment."

"I agree with you," I said, "but you and I are mature adults. Adolescent kids don't think like that. Remember, most kids don't really think far ahead. They live for the moment. They don't think they're going to get caught, and if they do think about it, they think the risk is worth it. Planning and rationality are years away for them.

THREE TYPES OF KIDS GET INVOLVED IN GANGS

"The way I see it, there are three kinds of kids who get involved in gangs. First, you have the kids who don't understand there are consequences to their actions. Second, you have the kids who understand there are consequences but are willing to take the risk. And third, you have the kids who understand the consequences and just don't care."

TYPE 1: KIDS WHO DON'T UNDERSTAND THERE ARE CONSEQUENCES TO THEIR ACTIONS

"But how can kids not understand there are consequences for their actions?" Robert asked.

KIDS DON'T KNOW THEY'RE DOING ANYTHING WRONG

"Sometimes they just don't think they're doing anything wrong. As we've seen in David's story tonight, most offenders usually drift into criminal behaviour – a lot of them don't realize what they are doing. Because they've been causing trouble for so long and getting away with it, the line between mischief and crime can get a little blurry. I've arrested kids who were totally surprised they were doing anything criminal.

"Last week I caught a kid spray-painting the side of an office building. He was doing it right in front of me. I was in uniform and he didn't care at all that I was watching. When I arrested him he was shocked. Defacing property had become totally normal for him. In music videos he saw kids spraying graffiti on public buildings all the time. He had lost all perspective, he thought graffiti was cool. For some kids crime is just part of their daily lives.

KIDS DON'T KNOW WHAT THEY ARE CAPABLE OF

"Another reason kids don't understand that there are consequences for their actions is the fact that many of them have no idea what they are capable of. We once had an emergency call to go to a subway station. One kid had given another youth a roundhouse kick and busted his jaw. When the police got there, the kid who did the kicking was cradling the victim in his arms, terrified the kid was going to swallow his tongue and choke to death. He couldn't believe what he had done. When we questioned him it was obvious he had no intention of causing this much harm. He didn't know how much damage a kick like that could cause. It was something he'd seen in the movies and in video games for years, where the victim never gets hurt. He had no concept of real-life violence until it happened. Youths generally feel that nothing can harm them and that what they do will have no lasting consequences. And what's more, the two kids at the subway were fighting over a cigarette.

TYPE 2: KIDS WHO UNDERSTAND THERE ARE CONSEQUENCES BUT ARE WILLING TO TAKE THE RISK

"As for the kids who understand the consequences but accept the risk, you have to remember they're acting in a gang and are sharing the responsibility and the risk.

SHARING THE RESPONSIBILITY AND THE RISK

"In a swarming, for example, there are so many kids involved that no single kid feels responsible – it's a watering down of accountability. And if they don't feel responsible for the harm or damage, they of course don't think they are risking much.

THE BENEFITS ARE WORTH THE RISKS

"Another thing to keep in mind is the fact that for a lot of kids the benefits of gang behaviour are huge. For them violence is a way of gaining status. A kid who beats up another kid, or slashes him with a knife becomes a hero in his gang – he is tough, cool. The rise in status is all the offender is thinking about, and the chance of getting caught is worth the risk.

WHAT RISKS?

"Keep in mind the attitude some kids have toward the Young Offenders Act. We'll talk more about this in future meetings, but for now, I want to say that a lot of kids think the Young Offenders Act is a joke. They simply don't believe they'll get caught or punished – they can't even imagine it.

TYPE 3: KIDS WHO UNDERSTAND THE CONSEQUENCES AND JUST DON'T CARE

"The third type – the ones who simply don't care are the worst. They have no empathy for their victims and they don't even care about themselves. For the type 1 and type 2 kids, there's hope. In some cases it's a matter of education – teaching them about the consequences, that the consequences are real, that they are hurting other people as well as themselves. When kids are young, parents should always ask, 'How would you feel if this happened to you?' This helps develop the maturity necessary to empathize with others. The type 3 kids were never socialized in this way. They are the most difficult ones to help."

LEAVING A GANG

Lydia put up her hand and when I nodded at her she said, "But for the kids who have the capacity to care, don't they eventually want to quit the gang when they realize their behaviour is doing damage?"

"You're right," I said, "some kids do wake up and see on their own that the gang life is wrong. Sometimes that happens when a kid matures. He just outgrows the gang. Those are the lucky ones. For the rest, the gang life comes to an end when we arrest them and they go to jail."

"What happens when a kid decides to leave his gang? Do the other members give him trouble?" Lydia asked.

"That's a good question. And the answer depends on what type of gang he is a member of. If he is just palling around with friends and is part of one of these loose groups, then most likely he will have no trouble leaving. Membership in these types of associations shifts all the time. So leaving is no big deal. However, if the gang is more formal and organized as it is in the hard-core street gangs, then things are much more serious. These gangs don't like deserters, and kids who leave or try to leave

65

generally receive threats. Some very organized gangs have their members fill out forms with the addresses of their relatives, and if the kid tries to leave, these relatives receive threats. The kids who try to leave these types of gangs are terrified of the consequences, and even if they do manage to leave, many of them are constantly looking over their shoulder. Remember, though, physically leaving a gang is a lot easier than psychologically leaving a gang. The gang members are — or at least were — their friends, and the gang life met many of their needs. Those needs still have to be met. If they aren't fulfilled, these kids will feel the tug to join the gang again.

DRIFT: GANGS AND THE VIOLENCE LADDER

"I think that covers it for gangs tonight. Let's move on and discuss the Violence Ladder and how it relates to David and his particular gang.

"With our earlier stories, we saw how the Violence Ladder can move from the initial harassment to serious violence in a matter of days. With David's story, the steps took much longer and happened over a period of months. But the length of time is not the key difference here. In the stories of Jamie and Rick, and Chris and Stick, the victim – or in the case of Chris, the victim who became an offender – was confronted by an already established gang.

"In David's case, however, we see a gang gradually forming as a reaction to an initial act of harassment. This slow version of the Violence Ladder in which kids come together and eventually form a gang is an example of what is sometimes called 'drift' by many researchers. Drift is unintentional gang formation. It's not always directly in response to the Violence Ladder. Sometimes kids form gangs because they just happen to be hanging out together, going to the same school, living in the same neighbourhood. Over time they form tight bonds and start getting into mischief together – eventually they start committing crimes. In this type of drift, the Violence Ladder emerges out of the group itself. It wasn't started, so to speak, by an outside group.

"I see David's drift into a gang as being a response to an outside act of harassment – the initial spark for all of his bad behaviour was the harassment and threats from Jerry on the first day of school which made him panic. They made David feel vulnerable, and gave him a need to reach out. Unfortunately, he sought support from his friends, not his parents. This is common and a major reason why grade nines get into trouble. They don't choose their friends wisely, and don't act as individuals. After Jerry kicked David and Gary out of the party, the two boys met another pair of boys, and together they all took their frustration out on a number of cars, keying the side doors. This was the beginning of David's drift into a gang. He never planned to get involved in a gang – it just happened. After this first act of vandalism, David and his friends moved to the minor offense of shoplifting, and from that to drugs, and then from drugs to assault. Each step seemed to just glide right into the next. There was no predetermined direction – they were drifting into trouble. David didn't plan to become a violent criminal, but that's exactly what happened–"

"Kevin," cut in Lydia, "I don't mean to interrupt, but I got the impression that peer pressure had a lot to do with why David acted like he did."

"Sure," I replied. "Certainly peer pressure has a lot to do with it, and there are other psychological factors involved. In David's case, he shared secrets with his friends which became the foundation of their friendship. Because they all shoplifted together, they had to trust each other to keep the secret. And as David told me, they all got an illicit thrill from breaking the law and not getting caught.

"I think it's important to get a bird's-eye view of what's happening before we start going inside these kids' heads. And when we stand back and look at why David formed a gang and why he acted violently, we see an obvious connection to the Violence Ladder. In the various stories I've told you in the past few months, we've seen how small incidents can easily erupt into serious violence. At each step along the way, the stakes get higher. The kind of violence our kids are involved in doesn't appear out of nowhere. Behind their acts of violence, you will usually see the Violence Ladder in operation. And the same goes for the formation of gangs. Most gangs don't just suddenly appear. They form gradually, over time.

"There is a relationship between gang formation and the Violence Ladder. The two often happen in parallel. In the case of David, the escalation of violence was instigated by Jerry and perpetuated by David and his friends. In the months following the initial harassment, David and his friends drifted into more and more trouble, becoming tighter and tighter along the way. By the time they met Jerry again months later, they were a group with a lot of history and strong bonds. David probably wouldn't see it as a gang – but that's not the point. They were committing crimes and therefore they were a gang. So at the second party, when they banded together and decided to exact revenge, the consequences were very serious – both for Jerry and for David. You see, the first act of harassment was never forgotten. Kids can carry grudges forever. Things are never left alone – that's why small events escalate into serious violence. These kids never let go. They don't walk away from things.

"The point I want to make is simply that the Violence Ladder is part of the gang phenomenon. In some way, the Violence Ladder is the engine that drives the formation of gangs. So, when we try to break the Violence Ladder, we'll also go a long way toward solving the gang problem.

"Together, these two phenomena have incredible transformative powers. Look how they changed a good student from a good family into a violent offender–"

Wendy put up her hand and then said, "Okay, I think I get it. You're saying there are these two forces at work – the Violence Ladder and gang formation – and that together they can make a kid do these violent things. But that's like saying these kids are helpless, that they're just victims of these invisible forces –"

"I'm not saying they're helpless. What I'm trying to show you is the underlying pattern. These kids aren't just acting randomly, they are following predictable patterns. And if we can recognize those patterns early on, we can step in and try to stop the inevitable violence. That's what we'll be focusing on next year – trying to break the Violence Ladder. But you're right — these kids aren't being blindly knocked around like billiard balls – they're responding to recognizable forces. Something inside them is urging them on. Like you mentioned before, the need to be accepted by their peers is certainly a key. And again, when we talk about solving the problem of violence next year, we'll see that addressing those needs is crucial. . . . So, why don't we spend a few moments now trying to get inside David's head and figure out why he turned to his friends for help, instead of his family? What did he get out of being in a gang? What needs were being met?"

DAVID'S GANG WAS LIKE A FAMILY

Wendy spoke up, "If you ask me, I think David had emotional needs that should have been met by his family, but instead were met by his gang of friends. In a sense, I think David's gang became sort of like a family in its own right. They were spending almost all their time together. They weren't going to anybody else for guidance or support."

Suddenly Robert threw up his hands and said, "Oh, come on. I think you're making a big deal out of this gang thing. I mean, really, this was just four deadbeat kids hanging around together and getting into trouble. . . that's it. And this idea that they're a kind of family doesn't wash with me."

A few parents seemed to nod in agreement with Robert. But other parents were shaking their heads. One of them, Mary, raised her hand and said, "Well, to me they do seem sort of like a family. They stick together, they trust each other and offer companionship – what's the difference?" she asked, looking over at Robert pointedly.

Holding up my hand I decided to wade into the argument. "Actually, Robert, I think Mary and Wendy are right. Groups like the one David and his friends formed are indeed like a family. David obviously didn't feel comfortable going to his parents for support. They weren't really involved in his life. The people who knew him best were his friends. So, when threatened by Jerry, instead of going to his parents, David turned to his friends. They were there to help him out. They offered him some badly needed support, but more than that, they filled an emotional vacuum in his life. You see, although David's parents loved him very much and tried to give him everything he wanted or needed, he could almost be seen as a neglected kid. His parents are both tied to demanding careers, sometimes working twelve-hour days, six or seven days a week, which means they don't see a lot of their kids. Whenever a kid is deprived of the attention he needs at home, he is susceptible to the lure of gangs. As nasty as gangs are, they adequately provide the attention that is missing at home. In his small group of friends, David found constant attention. There was always some-one to do something with, and always someone who was interested in him. You could even read David's criminal behaviour as a cry for attention. In the end, crying in jail, David got more attention from his parents in one night than he'd had in two months.

"I should add that I find a certain amount of irony with wealthy families when their kids get in trouble. I say this because few parents in these families ever consider that their kids are capable of getting into trouble. This means that the kids are given lots of freedom, and sometimes lots of money. Freedom and money in the hands of a bored kid, especially one who feels as lost and alone as David did in his new high school, is trouble waiting to happen.

SUMMARY

"Okay," I said, "we've reached the end of our meeting for tonight. Let's just quickly summarize what we've learned about gangs. First, a gang is any group of three or more youths who come together and commit illegal acts. Gangs do not necessarily resemble the hard-core gangs we see in the movies, so we have to throw out the stereotype of the hardened gang kid from the ghetto running around with an Uzi. Second, the four types of gang behaviour are vandalism and tagging, harassment, extortion, and violence. Third, kids get many benefits from being in a gang, such as popularity, protection, a sense of family, identity, self-esteem, power and material things.

"Next month's story involves two gangs – but this time the members are all girls, and I think you'll be shocked by their behaviour. We'll spend some time talking about girls and gangs and how they compare to the boys gangs. Then we'll explore the problem of youth violence in Canada."

6

GIRLS AND GANGS

Mary was the first parent to arrive to the December meeting. "I'm glad I caught you before we start," she said. "Actually I was very interested in last month's story about David and his friends, because I had a situation at home at the beginning of this school year that introduced me to the whole gang phenomenon. . . ."

"Something serious?" I asked.

"Well, it could have been," she replied. "My daughter Karen is in grade eight. You know how kids are around that age — not yet in high school, not quite a teenager, but still thinking that they're all grown up."

"Especially the girls," I said. "I really notice a difference in the maturity levels between boys and girls around the time they're just hitting puberty."

"Well, a friend of my daughter's named Rachel ran into a few problems with some other kids at school, and instead of doing what you've been suggesting, and reporting the harassment or bullying or whatever to a teacher or principal, she thought she could handle the problem by herself. I've met Rachel many times and she always seemed like such a nice girl to me. She used to spend a lot of time with Karen – they met in grade six and have spent the last couple of summers going to camp, playing volleyball and swimming and stuff.

"But then Rachel started getting picked on by some of the other kids. Like I said, she didn't report it, and instead she surrounded herself with all of her friends for protection. She wanted Karen to join her group – which really sounded more like a gang to me – and that's when I found out about the whole thing.

71

"I told Karen to forget it. No way was she going to be fighting at school. So I called the principal, and right away he called all the kids involved into his office. He told them he wouldn't tolerate this kind of behaviour on school property. He did a great job of diffusing the situation, and Karen, luckily, stayed out of trouble. Mostly, I think, because she had the good sense to come and speak to me."

"That's good to hear, Mary," I said. "Keep that story in mind when you hear what I have to say at tonight's meeting. I'll actually be telling a story very similar to that, but one that turned into something more serious. It'll be an eye-opener."

By this time, the other parents had arrived so I walked to the front of the class and began, "Tonight, I'm going to tell you a story about two girl gangs. This will give us a chance to explore girls and gangs in general. Then we'll take a break and come back and discuss how youth violence has increased over the past 10 years, how big the problem is in Canada, and how many weapons are in our schools and communities.

LENORE

"The story I want to relate this evening involves a girl named Lenore, who was in grade ten when I first met her. The other kids at her high school described her as aggressive and manipulative. She was good at picking out passive, introverted kids and imposing her will on them. She was an accomplished professional when it came to leading a group and getting her own way. She was an ordinary-looking kid, tall for her age, with thick black hair, not especially well dressed, not wealthy or extraordinarily smart, but she certainly knew how to make things happen. To her, everything was a power struggle, a quest for more and more attention and respect from her classmates, because there is a great deal of status attached to being the toughest girl in school.

"For example, Lenore had once been involved in a running argument with another girl, Michelle, who lived in her neighbourhood. For weeks, Lenore harassed Michelle. With a group of silent but imposing friends to accompany her, Lenore would often follow Michelle home – just to intimidate her. She also spread malicious and completely untrue rumours, calling Michelle a slut and a drug addict. She threatened her repeatedly, eventually reducing her to tears in the school hallway. After two weeks, unable to take anymore of this unrelenting hassle, Michelle cracked – she broke down at home and cried to her parents and her brother. She told them she thought she was going to be killed. She said she couldn't face going to school anymore. That's when Michelle's brother, Michael, stepped in. Michael assured Michelle and their parents that he would take care of it.

"He came to school the next day and confronted Lenore alone in an empty hallway between classes. His protective instincts were in full force. He was mad and determined to get Lenore off his sister's back. Unfortunately, he hadn't considered the possibility that a girl would stand up to him. He thought that a simple, direct show of brute strength would scare Lenore off – frighten her into leaving his sister alone. So he grabbed Lenore, screamed at her to back-off and stay the hell away from Michelle. He expected tears and a stuttering apology, but got something else instead. Lenore easily broke away from his grip, reached into her purse and whipped out a short knife. Screaming, she dove at him and swung, cutting a deep gash in his arm. He ran down the hall trailing blood.

"Michael was too embarrassed to tell anyone what happened. He told the school infirmary he'd slipped and cut his arm on a piece of metal. Lenore, however, bragged about her feat. And pretty soon, she had a reputation around the school as a bad girl – someone you don't mess with.

KATHY AND LENORE'S STORY

"Eventually, Lenore's behaviour led to a gang problem. From what we were able to learn from interviews with the kids who were involved, the gang incident started when Lenore overheard an after-school conversation between a girl named Kathy, who was also in grade ten, and Lenore's boyfriend, Earl. Apparently Kathy and Earl were chatting about an upcoming biology test, trading guesses at the type of questions they'd be asked, and laughing about what assignments they hadn't done. But Lenore didn't bother to check into that. All she saw was another woman making a move on her territory.

"Lenore didn't interrupt Kathy and Earl, she didn't even confront her boyfriend later about what she thought was inappropriate behaviour. Instead, she secretly sought revenge.

"Soon after her innocent conversation with Earl, Kathy started hearing from kids in her grade that Lenore was going to get her. Lenore had the rumour mill fired up. Her friends were dropping not-so-subtle hints to Kathy every time they saw her – telling her that she was going to get her 'ass kicked.' After school, while working on her homework in the safety of her bedroom, she began to receive calls – anonymous messages warning her that she would die soon. Like Michelle from the year before, Kathy found herself being followed home from school. She became scared, then frightened, then absolutely terrified. She knew the stories about Lenore. She figured there was nowhere to turn for help. She felt trapped and alone.

"Instead of talking to her parents, or going to the school authorities or the police for help, Kathy tried to deal with the problem on her own, in the only way she could think of – she formed a gang. And in the process she made the switch from innocent victim to potential offender.

"Although she was motivated only by the need to protect herself, Kathy dug herself deeper into a hole of terror and confusion. She didn't have a background of assault or a pattern of manipulative behaviour to draw on like Lenore. She was a good kid from a decent home, but she was scared and she thought the only way to stop Lenore's harassment was to turn to her friends and meet aggression with aggression. So Kathy and her friends marched the halls of the school in a pack. They walked to school together in the mornings and left together at night. At lunch they all sat together in the cafeteria. Kathy figured there was safety in numbers, and hoped that Lenore would give up once she saw that Kathy had a gang of her own.

"But Kathy soon realized how wrong she was. Her 'gang' was made up of kids like her – not criminals, not hard kids pumped full of attitude, ready to strike out at anybody who provoked them. Kathy's gang didn't try to harass Lenore or any of her friends, they didn't hit anybody, they weren't carrying weapons. They were just trying to scare Lenore off. But, instead of providing protection for Kathy, the kids in Kathy's gang began to find themselves the target of Lenore's harassment. Lenore's gang started bullying and threatening Kathy's friends. Within days, Kathy's gang fell apart. Lenore's divide-and-conquer approach worked quickly and easily. It was at this point that Kathy, exhausted and frightened, finally turned to the police.

"Her eight-page confession led to Lenore's suspension. Fortunately, and as is often the case, Lenore's gang splintered without her 'leadership' and the problem was essentially solved.

THE VIOLENCE LADDER

"Let's take a look at how the Violence Ladder applies to Kathy and Lenore's story. As well, let's discuss girls and gangs in general and how boys and girls are different.

"In last month's story about David, the kid who assaulted Jerry at a party, we saw a unique example of the Violence Ladder – what is sometimes called drift. After being harassed or threatened, David felt vulnerable and sought support among his friends. His intention wasn't to literally form a gang, but after hanging out with his friends on the street and getting into mischief with them, that's what happened. Within a few months, he had what I would call a gang. In Lenore and Kathy's story, we see a new gang forming, but this time it isn't drift. Kathy's gang is no accident. She intentionally forms her own gang in response to Lenore's harassment and threats. But, as usual, the Violence Ladder is behind it all." I looked around the room at the faces of the parents. "Can anyone here give us a run-through of how Kathy and Lenore moved up the various steps of the Violence Ladder?"

A few hands went up, including Mary's. "Let me see if I've got this straight," she began. "Lenore got the wrong idea when she saw Kathy talking to Earl – who was Lenore's boyfriend, right? So, Lenore set out to get revenge. Her friends began to harass Kathy – which is the first step on the Violence Ladder. Kathy didn't report it to anyone – which allowed the escalation to continue. And, so, it was at that point that things began to escalate. Lenore stepped up her harassment. She started calling Kathy at home and became more threatening and belligerent, which is the second step. Then, I guess Kathy got scared and, since she didn't feel she could tell anyone, she formed her own gang for protection. That was grouping, which is step three, and it raised the stakes. But instead of backing off, Lenore's girls reacted by bullying and harassing the members of Kathy's gang. Luckily, I guess, Kathy finally had the sense to call the police and the Violence Ladder was broken before there was serious violence."

"Excellent, Mary!" I said, "Good job. And just so that we're all clear – remember that the escalation usually goes from harassment to threats to grouping to weapons to violence. Luckily, in this case, the Violence Ladder was broken before anyone resorted to weapons use or serious violence."

GIRLS, VIOLENCE AND GANGS

Wendy put her hand up and said, "Kevin, is the problem with girls a serious one, or are girls like Lenore really only an exception?"

"Yes, I think the problem with girls is serious, and there are lots of other girls like Lenore out there. Many of them are serious gang members who carry weapons, deal in drugs, and who are not shy about committing any number of crimes. In September 1995, a *Globe & Mail* article entitled "Girl-Gang Violence Alarms Experts" reported on a Women in Canada report released by Statistics Canada. The report said that one quarter of all youths charged with violent offenses in 1993 were girls. And they commit their fair share of property offenses as well: one fifth of those charged with property offenses in 1993 were girls. Still, it is true that far fewer girls are gang members than boys. A commonly accepted figure is that one in fourteen gang members is a girl. You might think that's low, but they're getting into trouble proportionately more often than the boys. Although far fewer gang members are girls, at least one of every five youths arrested in Canada is a girl."

Lydia seemed eager to ask a few questions. I nodded in her direction and she spoke up. "Do these girls just form their own gangs like Lenore and Kathy, or do they also join existing gangs with boys in them?" she asked.

"They're doing both. Girls will join existing boys gangs that don't mind having girls in them. But we are seeing more and more all-girl gangs."

THE DIFFERENCE BETWEEN BOYS AND GIRLS

"Are there any major differences between what girls do and what boys do?" Lydia asked.

"Yes. In general, boys have problems with other boys, and girls with other girls. In other words, girls are victims mostly at the hands of other girls. Another big difference is the fact that we don't often see the all-out gang rivalries we sometimes find in the male gangs where two gangs constantly compete against each other. Occasionally that happens with the girls, like when two rival girl gangs come to blows in the school yard and a big fight breaks out – they call them 'cat fights' and they tend to draw a large crowd of spectators. But that doesn't happen a lot. Most of the time, it's one gang of girls picking on a single individual. They'll stalk her in the halls, intimidate her, call her names, spread rumours about her, threaten her, and they'll keep up this kind of harassment for weeks, months even. That's what Lenore's gang did to Kathy. Girls are much more tenacious than boys. Boys don't have the patience for these long, drawn-out campaigns – they're much more likely to resort to violence. In fact, I would say that the most striking difference between boys and girls is that boys are much more physical, whereas girls are more psychological.

PSYCHOLOGICAL WARFARE

"Some girls like Lenore have an uncanny ability to play psychological games. They know how to hurt people without using force. They know what buttons to push – exactly what to say to really get at somebody. Sometimes they don't say anything – they'll just stare another girl down. They even have a word for it – they call it giving somebody 'cut-eye.'

"Often, the psychological damage from harassment and threats is worse than physical injury. I say this because the victim is often scared and anxious for weeks or even months. They suffer all day long, not knowing when the threat might be carried out. The victim is always looking over their shoulder, losing sleep and even skipping school. Unfortunately, psychological harassment is difficult to stop. That's our major problem when dealing with girls. As most people know, verbal or mental terrorization often doesn't get reported because the victims are afraid and they don't think anyone can help them. Even if an incident is reported, the offense is often hard to prosecute.

WHEN GIRLS GET PHYSICAL

"However, as we've seen with Lenore and the knife, girls are not afraid of resorting to violence if the situation calls for it. In fact, we're finding that girls are often more vicious than boys. At school, a girl gang will yank its target into an empty classroom and start tugging her hair out, scratching

77

her face, and biting her, whereas boys will usually only punch and kick. And because girls fight like this, the damage they do is often more serious than that done by boys.

"Another important thing to understand about girls is that we're not used to seeing them act violently, and the girls that commit violent acts are very aware of this. They know they can get away with a lot simply because people have trouble accepting aggressive girls. They daringly abuse people in public. They know they are catching everybody off their guard. A few weeks ago, for instance, a group of 15-year-old girls were traveling the subway together in a pack after school. They were threatening and beating up other girls, then stealing their coats or Walkmans, and they were doing all this in front of a large crowd of rush-hour commuters and a number of transit employees. Nobody intervened because they all thought it was just a few girls having an argument. You see, because they were female everyone assumed it wasn't a dangerous situation, and that's just not true – as the victims will attest."

GIRLS AGAINST BOYS

"So, do girls only target other girls? Do you ever see girls attacking boys?" asked Lydia.

"As I've said, generally girls pick on other girls, but they certainly have no trouble standing up to a boy. We saw that with Lenore when she was faced with Michelle's brother. In fact, a lot of guys are terrified of girls. I mean some of these girls are bigger and stronger than them. In some cases they're carrying knives and sometimes guns, as well. The thing is, anybody with a weapon can be terrifying. I've seen some guys get totally beaten up by a bunch of girls. These girls aren't afraid. They punch and kick the hell out of the guys. They can be really vicious. I think some of them go out of their way to be really brutal, just so people will take them seriously."

Robert mumbled from his seat at the back. "Don't the guys fight back?"

"A lot of them are reluctant to fight. There's still a sense that it's not fair, and I guess a guy would be worried about his image. His friends won't think he's tough if he beats up a girl."

"That's kind of a double standard then," Robert remarked.

"In my experience," I said, "they won't fight back, so they just take it. And getting beat up by girls is really embarrassing for them, so they hush the thing up as much as possible. We know that guys are getting assaulted by girls, but we rarely hear about it. They often don't report it because they feel it won't be taken seriously."

"So if the boys don't fight back, then the girls aren't afraid of them. I mean, you don't see girls getting hurt by boys, do you?" Wendy asked.

"Girls are certainly more worried about being victimized by other girls than by boys, except in tragic cases of sexual assault. Unfortunately, the topic of sexual assault deserves more attention than we can give it at these meetings.

Summary

"Before we take a break, let me summarize the points we've made about girls and gangs. First, we learned that the problem with girls is serious – one quarter of all youths charged with violent offences in 1993 were girls. Second, we discussed the difference between girls and boys. A lot of the abuse inflicted by girls is psychological, whereas the abuse from boys is usually physical. Third, we saw that when girls do become physical they can be much more vicious than boys. They will pull someone's hair out, scratch their face and bite them, whereas boys will usually only punch and kick.

"When we return, we'll discuss the actual statistics that tell us how large the problem of youth violence is."

7

A Picture Of Youth Violence

" Let's move onto the statistics," I said. "I promise to keep it short and simple, so, I'll share with you 3 things – no more. We could drown in statistics and reports very quickly if we aren't focused. There are volumes of data out there, but as far as we're concerned there are 3 key points: one – youth violence has increased dramatically over the last 10 years; two – even though the crime rate slightly decreased last year, youth violence is still a big problem in Canada; and three – there are gangs and weapons in our schools and communities.

POINT 1: YOUTH VIOLENCE HAS INCREASED DRAMATICALLY OVER THE LAST 10 YEARS

"Recently the Canadian Centre for Justice Statistics released their annual crime figures for 1994 and the numbers have led many people to conclude that the amount of youth crime in Canada is actually decreasing. In the newspapers, analysts claim the public is overreacting. They say we're panicking and youth violence is not as big a problem as we think. And yet on a daily basis we see sensational stories of violent crimes being committed by children. We hear parents and children speaking out against youth violence and we hear of studies and reports showing just how serious a problem we have. It's a confusing and very serious situation.

"Basically, I feel that, if even one child is hurt by another, we have a problem that needs to be solved. I think that's something we all agree on and we should keep that in mind as we try to evaluate the statistics on youth violence, because numbers can distract us from the real issues. Although the analysts would say statistics are objective and unbiased – that numbers never lie – I would disagree. I think spending too much time worrying over a few small percentage points in the overall crime rate can cause us to forget that these are children we're talking about. Our children. Behind each percentage point in the youth homicide reports is a real child who went to school, played sports, had a family and friends and is now dead.

"The 1994 stats from the Canadian Centre for Justice Statistics do show that the number of youth crimes dropped 5% from 1993 and violent episodes specifically, were down 2% from the year before. But, as I said, I think it would be foolish to believe the problem is going away based on those numbers.

"Crime may have slipped a little in the past few years, but that really is more of a blip than a major trend. Remember, throughout the '80s crime soared at an alarming rate– a rate that was bound to taper off eventually. Before this little dip, crime rose steadily for 15 years straight. And, even when you factor in the drop that occurred in 1994, overall crime is still 8% higher than it was 10 years ago. However, between 1986 and 1994 the rate of violent crime committed by youth went up 133.5% across Canada, according to Stats Can's 1996 *Canadian Crime Statistics* report. That's the situation we are attempting to address at these meetings. Remember the first of the three most important points you need to know about youth violence – our children's world is radically different from the one we grew up in.

THINGS WILL CONTINUE TO GET WORSE

"Not only has the amount of youth violence grown since we were kids but I feel it will continue to grow worse for some time to come."

At that point Wendy put up her hand. "Actually Kevin, I remember reading an article in *The Atlantic Monthly* on youth violence," she said. "I think the July 1995 issue had an entire feature on crime trends. I know *The Atlantic* is a US publication and their figures are American, but I wonder if what's happening in the States might be applicable to us here in

Canada. The article said that even though the total number of teenagers has dropped in the past 10 years, they've been getting more and more violent, and crime has been rising. In particular, over the past few decades, the homicide rate has doubled for kids aged fourteen to seventeen. And the teenage population is about to bulge! In ten years, the population of kids aged fourteen to seventeen will rise nearly 25 percent."

I agreed, "The population might be aging, but we're still going to see an increase in the total number of young people in our own country. That's alarming if you consider that a 1995 *Globe and Mail* article reported that although teenagers made up 11% of the population in 1994, they were responsible for 20% of the violent crimes. These are the children of the baby-boomers. And, yes, if we look to the States as an indicator of where we might be in a few years, as many experts do, the picture looks bleak indeed. For instance, a study that came out of the Washington Department of Justice in 1992, showed that the incidence of rape, robbery, or assault among juveniles was five times greater in that year, than it was among adults 35 or older. In the same year, the US Office of Juvenile Justice and Delinquency Prevention reported that one out of every thirteen juveniles was a victim of a violent crime.

"That's why we're preparing for more crime, not less," I added.

POINT 2: EVEN THOUGH THE CRIME RATE MAY DECREASE IN THE SHORT TERM, YOUTH VIOLENCE IS STILL A BIG PROBLEM IN CANADA

Robert put his hand up, "I don't get it. I know that over the long term our kid's world has become more violent. But you just told us that there was a decrease in the youth crime rate last year. Doesn't that mean that things are getting better?"

"Sure, a little," I replied, "but the youth violence problem is still very serious. So what if two percent fewer kids were stabbed from one year to the next? In absolute terms that means that there were 23,374 violent offences in 1993 and 'only' 23,010 in '94. That's still horrible. Again, when you focus on percentages and numbers I think we lose sight of the value and quality of individual life. What happens to those 23,000 victims? What about their parents, friends, brothers and sisters? Do we ignore them and next year's potential 22,646 victims because the crime rate is trending down by 364 beatings a year. That's ridiculous. You have to ask yourself when your number's going to be up.

"I'm not the kind of cop who sits behind a desk. I'm out there talking to the kids. And I would say that things are worse today than they were a generation ago and I think that people who hear overall crime is down and then feel it's okay to walk the streets at night are wrong. I mean, even if crime really is down this year, isn't that like saying, 'Don't worry, your flooded basement's okay, there's only five feet of water down there, not six.' Thousands of kids are still getting punched, stabbed, or shot. What if you found out there were only three rapists on your street instead of five, would you suddenly feel safe?

"I guess the point I'm trying to make is simply that a 3% drop in the violent crime rate doesn't mean we have this problem sorted out — not by a long shot. One or two years out of a fifty-year trend is statistically insignificant. As I've already said, between 1986 and 1994, violent crime committed by young offenders increased 133.5%. When it goes down 133.5% I'll start to smile.

"When you look at crime stats, you should keep in mind what every police officer, educator or researcher knows – crime stats are just the tip of the iceberg. A lot of stuff goes unreported. A lot of victims keep their mouths shut. And they have their reasons for being quiet – fear of retaliation, or figuring that their complaint won't be taken seriously, for instance. And, as I've said before, a lot of the bad youth behaviour is not necessarily illegal, or even if it is, like verbal intimidation or physical abuse, some kids might not realize that a crime has been committed – so they don't report it. Certainly the other borderline stuff, like being quietly followed, would never get reported. So, intimidation and harassment continue to eat away at the school environment. This is what gets missed by the media. We're not talking about sensational murders – we're talking about intimidation and fear, the whole underbelly of stuff that goes on unnoticed, the stuff that affects our kids on a daily basis.

WHAT OUR CHILDREN SAY ABOUT YOUTH VIOLENCE

"You only have to ask your children how they feel about it and you will see that this is true. And, actually, we do have a good idea of what the kids are thinking. A few studies have been done and, of course, officers like me are in the schools talking to them everyday. For instance, a 1994 study of over 950 students done by the Canadian Research Institute for Law and the Family on behalf of the Calgary Police Service asked what kinds of things children were worried about at school. Close to 75% of the students were worried they would get something stolen. Over half were worried that someone will threaten to hurt them, and just under half of them were worried that someone would punch or kick them, or that a gang would beat them up. It's an unfortunate blessing that as adults we have less reason to fear young criminals – most of the victims of youth crime are youths themselves."

At the back of the room Mike's hand suddenly shot up. "Sure," he said, "but being worried about something is one thing, having it happen is another."

"I think the worrying is enough. If that's how the kids feel then it's certainly affecting their ability to concentrate on their schoolwork," I said. "Furthermore, it's not like these children are worrying for no reason. The researchers also asked the students what kinds of things they had experienced personally. Over 80% of them said they were a victim of at least something. Over half said they had something stolen. Over 40% said they had been threatened, and nearly 40% said they had been slapped or kicked. 6% said they had been attacked by a group or gang. This last figure is a good example of the fear factor. Fortunately the number of kids who said they got attacked by a gang is a lot lower than the number who said they worried about it, but the fact they worry about it means they don't feel safe. I should add that this survey asked the kids to answer the questions both in terms of when they were at school and when they were outside school. In nearly every case, students said they were more worried about being victims while at school. And as far as being victims went, considerably more were victimized at school, as opposed to outside of school – over eighty percent compared to under seventy. So, wandering the streets and roaming around downtown are perceived to be safer activities than walking the halls of their schools."

I stopped and took a sip of water. "Before we move on I should point out that the Calgary study was done in 1994. The information is valid and I do think it is worthwhile looking at this study because it shows how a large number of students from a number of different schools think. We should take what the kids say seriously.

"But my personal belief is that if we redid the same study tomorrow in the schools that I visit we would see very different results. Some areas have dealt with youth violence quite well over the past few years. I think that Ontario now has some very effective youth violence programs like Zero Tolerance, Peer Mediation and Student Crime Stoppers. We'll look at those and many other programs in more detail at a later meeting. But they have been working. In my opinion, many schools are not as unsafe as they were a couple of years ago when the Calgary study was completed.

MOST KIDS ARE GOOD

"Our schools are not out of control, but many do have a problem with violence. It is important to remember what we talked about at our first meeting – most kids are good and only a small proportion of them are the troublemakers. Unfortunately the troublemakers ruin it for the rest. It's also important to remember that we can't divide the school body up into two categories: good kids and bad kids. A number of kids fall into a gray area. These kids are basically good, but are impressionable. You know the type – the good kid who starts running with the bad crowd and starts acting out. A good example of that is the story I told you in our second meeting, the one about Chris who ended up stabbing another kid at the subway. I worry a lot about this type of kid, because these are the offenders we can really do something about. They're impressionable both ways. Give them bad examples, and they'll go bad, but give them good examples and they'll do good. The really bad apples are hard to deal with. Many of them have problems that run so deep, there's not much we can do."

"So, how many kids actually misbehave?" Mary demanded.

"Well, the Calgary survey asked the students how many of them had ever engaged in at least one type of delinquent behaviour and, shockingly, nearly 75% said they had. Over half said they had done so within the past year."

"What kind of things were they doing?"

"Stuff like slapping or kicking someone, stealing a few bucks, threatening to hurt someone –"

I saw Mary's eyes roll. "You mean they're all bad."

"No," I replied. "Generally, most kids are good. I mean most kids are not responsible for the really serious stuff. I'm not surprised that most kids have done something bad. Some of that is kids just being kids. Even I shoplifted once. But the number is high because some school administrators allow for an atmosphere that tends to both promote and condone delinquency. In some schools fear is rampant and rules are lax or not enforced. Some kids take advantage of the fact that they won't get punished for misbehaving. They get away with a lot at school these days. Skipping classes is a breeze. They're not afraid of getting a detention. There's no feeling of accountability. That's why it's crucial for parents, police, and educators to form partnerships. When they work together, there are fewer problems, and when problems do occur, they are handled properly."

"But if you're saying that most kids are generally good, who's responsible for this climate of fear you keep talking about?" Mary asked.

A SMALL CORE OF BAD KIDS ARE RESPONSIBLE FOR A HIGH PERCENTAGE OF THE VIOLENCE

"A small, core group of bad kids which exists in most schools are most responsible for stirring things up. It's not easy to put a figure on what percentage of children might be the core offenders, but we've asked hundreds of school officials, police and students to give us estimates and their answers range from one or two percent of the students, to over ten. And, of course, it varies from school to school. Fred Mathews has come up with a helpful model. The numbers aren't supposed to be spot on, but they do give a basic understanding of the school dynamics. According to his model, five percent of the kids are what he calls 'high-risk,' the ones with problem backgrounds – victims of abuse, neglect, poverty. These kids are extremely vulnerable and are the ones responsible for the delinquency. But even within this five percent, Dr. Mathews figures there's a core of one or two percent who are behind the really violent stuff.

"Then, beyond this five-percent group of bad kids, there's another portion of twenty percent who are at moderate risk. The kids in this category are the ones who normally wouldn't do anything criminal, but have the tendency to do so when the circumstances are right. If they know they can get away with it, they'll go ahead and steal, or vandalize, or whatever. A lot of them are followers, taking their lead from the small core of violent students. Then you have the rest of the kids, the remaining seventy-five percent. Dr. Mathews calls these the 'low-risk' or 'no-risk' kids – kids with solid upbringings. Unfortunately, these are the ones that frequently end up as victims or innocent bystanders. Most of the time they never report what they see, so this helps create the atmosphere of fear.

"In addition to the fact that more kids are at risk of becoming offenders, there are two other trends we need to be aware of. Trend 1 is that both violent offenders and their victims are getting younger, and Trend 2 is that the acts of violence are getting more violent.

TREND 1: BOTH VIOLENT OFFENDERS AND THEIR VICTIMS ARE GETTING YOUNGER

"I was actually talking to some fellow police officers the other day about this problem, and we are all very worried. Each of us has started to see really young kids getting in trouble. I mean kids under twelve. A lot of them are ten or even nine years old. . . . A series of focus groups was recently conducted with police, teachers and kids across Canada. The findings, published in a booklet called *School Violence and the Zero Tolerance Alternative* by Thomas Gabor, Ph.D., showed that nearly half of the school staff interviewed felt that we had a moderate to major problem with kids under the age of twelve."

"What are these kids doing?" Wendy asked with concern in her voice.

"Same things as the older kids – harassment, verbal abuse, ganging up on each other. A lot of them are influenced by the older kids, who are their role models. In fact, the older kids exploit their celebrity status, so to speak, and 'use' the younger kids whenever they can."

"Use them?" Wendy asked.

"As runners, gophers. They get them to deliver stolen goods, that kind of thing. They figure using these kids is a way of avoiding calling attention to their activities. Who's going to suspect a nine-year-old of carrying stolen merchandise? And, even if you catch the nine-year-old, how are you going to punish him? Some of these under-twelve-year-olds are pretty wise about the system. They know they are free from the law. Under the current Young Offenders Act a child under the age of twelve cannot be charged with a crime. The older kids tutor them about this kind of thing. These gangs are pretty shifty."

"So, how young are some of these kids?" asked Mary.

"Well, we've seen grade-school kids forming cliques, which are like little seed gangs. And the problem with these young gangs is that the kids in them learn a lot about misbehaving. By the time they get to secondary school, they're experienced gang members – they know how to harass someone, how to steal, how to conceal weapons in their clothing. They're veterans at it.

"Last year, I heard about a bunch of grade-one kids ganging up on another kid and punching him out. One witness said the gang members were repeatedly banging the kid's head on the pavement. These are problem kids, and a lot of them show signs of aggression and anti-social behaviour as far back as kindergarten. In fact, The National Institute of Mental Health in the States is studying various early intervention programs with these types of kindergarten kids and is providing extra training on how to be social. The experts feel that, in order to be successful, it's imperative to reach aggressive children when they are young – and the younger, the better. This is important because social training with kids who are already in their teens is not always successful. The patterns of behaviour are often too entrenched to be changed. I'm not saying all kindergarten kids with behavioural problems turn out to be violent. But violent teenagers usually have a long history of problems – a history that begins in their early childhood."

"So, you can't even count on your kindergarten kid being safe," Mary said.

I shook my head glumly and then Jackie spoke up, looking over at Mary.

"Actually, Mary," she said, "my sister-in-law has a daughter in grade two, and they recently had a problem. Some of the other kids in her class began harassing her. At first they started calling her names, but then they got more aggressive and started to hit her. My sister-in-law flipped out when she heard what was going on. Fortunately, the principal and the parents of the other kids got involved and the harassment stopped – but it was pretty scary. I was alarmed too, to discover that kids this young can be that bad. So, Kevin's right – it does happen."

TREND 2: THE ACTS OF VIOLENCE ARE GETTING MORE VIOLENT

"The situation is very scary," I said. "And, unfortunately, there is also a second trend that is just as disturbing. Today's statistics show that young violent offenders are actually becoming more violent. And, connected to this we are seeing an increase in weapons use and gang activity in our schools and communities.

"In my job, I spend a lot of time looking at surveys and studies done by researchers, educators and police departments from across the country. I see it as my responsibility to the children and the parents to be well-informed and to keep up with the latest information on what's going on in our schools. Frankly, the results are heart-stopping. For instance, the Calgary study done by the Canadian Research Institute for Law and the Family that I mentioned earlier found that 4 out of 10 male students and 1 in 10 female students said they had carried some type of weapon to school in the past year. That's frightening when you compare it to your own youth. I remember when I was in high school, one kid carried a buck knife on his belt and used it to terrify all the other kids. But someone went to the principal's office, reported it, and right away, the kid with the buck knife was expelled. Now, personally, I don't think expulsion was necessarily the right solution, but it goes to show you how different the climate was back then. Violence was pounced upon when we were kids. But things have changed. As that Calgary study shows, violence is just no big deal for many kids these days.

"I don't mean to be alarmist, but groups and gangs are everywhere now. Sure, some schools are worse than others, and a lot of schools don't have much of a problem, but it is pervasive. I've spoken to parents who send their kids to private schools, and they all think, 'Well, my kid goes to a really safe school. All the kids are from very strict families, and they're well behaved and all,' – but these schools have their incidents too. Some of the schools don't like to admit it. You know, it's hard for a principal of a well-respected school to say, 'Hey, I think we should create awareness about students intimidating other students, or students vandalizing school property.' They don't want to send a message to the parents that says 'We have a problem.' But the reality is a lot of these schools do have a problem. Most of the time it's related to football games, or hockey games. There are countless stories of kids from one school ganging up on a player from another school, getting into his locker room and trashing his stuff. And often these incidents don't even make it into the school announcements.

"Having said that though, I have to tell you, the other day I got a call from a teacher at a private school. He wants me to come to the school and speak to the kids. That's a good sign. It takes guts for these high-priced schools to get a cop in the gymnasium speaking to the student body. In general, I am quite happy that educators are really opening up to the parents and the police. I think in the last few years school staff have realized the size and severity of the violence problem in their schools, and they recognize that the most effective way to handle violence is to deal with it openly – and that includes sharing responsibility with both parents and police."

POINT 3: THERE ARE GANGS AND WEAPONS IN OUR SCHOOLS AND COMMUNITIES

I looked to my left and saw Lydia's hand in the air. "Kevin," she said, "I'm confused about what we're actually discussing – you've talked about youth violence in general, but you've made the point several times that, these days, violence or harassment is rarely an individual act – most of your stories show kids banding together into gangs to commit crime. Do we have a gang problem in Canada just like they do in the U.S.?"

"In a recent *Globe and Mail* article the Metro Toronto Police estimated that 12% of the city's students are pressured to join gangs for self protection," I said, soberly.

"That's more than one in ten," Lydia said, raising her eyebrows.

"That's only the average. In some schools it's higher. Others, of course, don't have much of a problem."

"But how come it's not all over the newspapers? What you're telling me sounds like we have a huge problem going on and nobody's really talking about it. So is there really a huge problem or not?" Lydia asked.

"As I've said. We've already had disturbing incidents. Hundreds of them. We've even had drive-by shootings. Weapons are turning up in some schools on a regular basis. The ground work is being laid for a huge crime wave. The youth workers in this city are in fact preparing for a big eruption in youth violence."

"But still," Mary said, jumping into the argument, "it will never be as bad here in Canada as it is in the States. We've got more controls on things like guns."

WE HAVE A GUN PROBLEM

"We have different gun laws in Canada, but the lax controls in the States have serious repercussions here," I replied. "We have a gun problem, and it's growing. It's growing because gunrunners are smuggling in thousands of guns from south of the border and selling them here in Canada. Getting guns into the country is considered a joke by the smugglers, and the profit potential is huge. Toronto, for instance, is a giant market for guns. Some school kids are clamouring to buy them up. Our hospitals are dealing with more and more gunshot wounds, and in some parts of the city, it's not uncommon to hear the crack of a gun from your living room.

"Once it starts, it's hard to stop, because the gun cycle is vicious. If one kid ups the ante by sporting a gun, the other kids feel they also have to buy a gun to defend themselves. It's an arms race, and fifteen-year-olds don't think about their actions. If a kid's pride is wounded or if his life is threatened, he's not going to go away and meditate on it, he's going to react right then and there. There was a school in Detroit, where they had three shootings in a single day. . . . I've heard that every two hours one child in America is shot to death. Even if our problem is a fraction of that, it's a concern."

YOUTH VIOLENCE OCCURS IN CANADA FOR THE SAME REASONS AS IN THE UNITED STATES

"But, you're talking about the States. Canada is a very different country," Mary shot back. "I don't see how you can make that analogy."

"Yes, Canada is not as violent as the States," I said. "But I think we have to recognize that the stats and stories coming out of America are warning signs telling us that if we don't do something soon, things could get worse here. The United States has ten times more people than Canada so it's not surprising that their youth crime problem is so much greater. But the underlying reasons that youth violence occurs are the same in Detroit, Washington, Toronto and Moosejaw. And that is scary because it tells us that, unless we deal with the root causes of violent behaviour among our children, we will have a huge problem in a few years just like the United States."

GUNS AND OTHER WEAPONS

"Well, how many kids carry weapons, Kevin?" Wendy cut in.

"If you remember, just after our break, I mentioned the results from that survey in Calgary. In that survey, over 40% of the male students and just over 12% of the female students claimed to have carried a weapon on at least one occasion in the past year. My guess is that's fairly typical of the rest of Canada."

91

"Guns?" Wendy asked me, her face lit up with shock.

"Fortunately they're not all guns. Only 5% of the males said they brought some type of handgun to school at least once in the past year. The weapon of choice is the knife. 1 in 4 guys has had a knife at school. And in a lot of schools, knives are confiscated on a daily basis – pocket knives, switch blades, butterfly knives. Guns are definitely confiscated less frequently. A study called *Weapons Use in Canadian Schools* by Sandra Gail Walker, of Educon Research and Marketing Systems, found that most schools may only retrieve one or two a year from their students. But that figure can climb as high as one or two a month in some schools. We're also seeing clubs and bats, socks with billiard balls stuffed in them, golf clubs, dart guns, explosives, homemade weapons. . . replica type guns."

"Where are they getting these weapons?" Wendy asked.

"Wherever they can," I replied. "We even confiscate weapons that the kids are making in shop class."

"But the guns. Where are they getting them?"

"As I've said, the gun trade is a thriving business. In fact, a lot of the guns that we come across are ones the students have bought from schoolmates who deal in the black market. Others are stolen from someone's dad who has hunting rifles. They'll just saw off the barrel. Or, in many cases, parents even buy pellet guns for their kids. Often these .192 calibre weapons are replicas of real guns and, due to their ammunition size, they have the potential to really harm somebody."

"I'm just not getting it, Kevin," said Wendy, frowning. "What are these kids doing with guns? What do they use them for?"

"Well, the replica pellet guns for instance are often used by kids to intimidate other kids. When you're staring down the barrel of what looks like a .45 caliber gun or a magnum, you do whatever somebody says. These kinds of guns are pulled out during robberies and even during arguments or fights between kids. Sometimes kids carry them for protection. But most of the time they just brandish them. You know, they pull up their T-shirts to show other kids the gun tucked under their belts – just like in gangster movies. It's a fear tactic. Guns are also a status symbol in the schools. . . . By far the biggest damage done by guns and other weapons is the psychological harm they cause."

"So they're not really using these weapons then?" Wendy asked.

"Well, as I've said, we've had beatings and stabbings and gunshots, but most of the crime involving youth doesn't include weapons. Something like 90% is not weapons-related. About half of the reported youth crime is property-related. And in the schools, most of the physical violence takes the form of fights. Minor assaults. Weapons aren't usually used in these fights. But the fact that these weapons are around is terrifying. The more weapons around, the more violent crime we have."

"Is there an increase in the number of weapons in our schools?" Wendy asked.

"That's one of those statistical questions. We don't know for sure. Kids hide them in their knapsacks, or lockers or leave them in their cars in the parking lot, or strap them to their ankles. We just don't know how many weapons are actually present in Canadian schools right now. All I can tell you is whether or not the seizure of weapons in Canadian schools has increased. And the latest figures I have for that, from the *Weapons Use In Canadian Schools* report, tell me that from 1992 to 1993 seizures went up for all weapons except modified shotguns and martial-arts equipment. As far as I know, that trend has continued. . . . Personally, I think we're finding more weapons in the schools because the kids are trying to get away with more.

SUMMARY

"Why don't I wrap up here. As you remember, there are three main points to draw from the statistics on youth violence.

"First – youth violence has increased dramatically over the last 10 years. Although the overall crime rate has increased 8% since 1984, the rate at which youth crime is committed grew 133.5% from 1986 to 1994.

"Second – even though the crime rate may decrease in the short term, youth violence is still a big problem in Canada. In 1994-95 there were more than 23,000 violent crimes committed by young offenders. And that is just the tip of the iceberg – many more go unreported. As well, we saw that most youth crime is committed by a small percentage of kids who are hard-core offenders; violent offenders are getting younger every year; and the acts of violence that they commit are getting more violent.

"Third – there are gangs and weapons in our schools and communities. We learned that most violent acts are done by kids acting in gangs rather than acting alone. And we learned that many kids carry weapons.

The Calgary survey reported that over 40% of the male students and just over 12% of the female students claimed to have carried a weapon on at least one occasion in the past year. And although guns are found in our schools, we noted that the weapon of choice is the knife.

"If you only take one thing away from this evening, please remember that, no matter what the analysts tell you in the newspapers or on TV, youth violence is a serious problem. I talk to the kids. I deal with them everyday. I see what is happening in our schools, on our streets and in our families and it is serious. The criminologists can play with numbers all day long and make it look like anything they want. But many of them don't spend time with our children. Some of them aren't aware of all the issues. They don't hear the stories like the ones I have told you so far this year. I would challenge anyone who doesn't believe youth violence is a problem to go and spend time with the kids, to talk to the parents of a victim of youth violence or to the parents of an offender. I think they would quickly see the magnitude of the problem.

"Okay, over the past few months, we have managed to cover the first two of our three most important points to understand about youth violence. So, when we come back in the new year we'll be able to start working together to figure out some concrete solutions that you as parents can put into effect to protect your child from youth violence. At our January meeting we'll be exploring the warning signs to look for in your child's behaviour that indicate that he or she is a victim of youth violence."

PART 3

*Protecting
Your Kids*

8

NO MORE VICTIMS

❝ As I mentioned at our last meeting, our focus from now on will be on the third most important point to understand about youth violence – 'Parents can help protect their kids.' And we'll split this up into three sections. Our first section will be 'What you can do at home to protect your kids from becoming a victim.' Our second section will be 'What we can all do to reduce the number of offenders.' And lastly, our third section will be 'The Prevention Triangle: how parents, schools and police can work together to eliminate youth violence.' And we'll be spending a month on each section.

"So, tonight, our topic is 'What you can do at home to protect your kid from becoming a victim.' This is why you are here. Everything we have learned up to now is the foundation for this. Last year as we were discussing the stories of Jamie and Chris we came up with some good strategies for ensuring our kids are safe. Jamie was the kid who was harassed by bullies to buy a knife. Chris was the good student who stabbed another kid in the subway. We'll be talking more about these stories and the strategies we developed from them. And I'd like to continue coming up with more strategies, but before we do that, I think the first thing we should do is explore the signs that your kid is becoming a victim. Knowing these signs is crucial for any parent who wants to help protect their children.

KYLE'S STORY

"The story today will show us in quite specific detail what signs a parent should watch for. This particular story is one I know extremely well. It happened to very good friends of mine, Jack and Betty Unger. They have two kids. Julie is five years old now and Kyle is twelve. This happened last year when Kyle was in grade six.

"I remember seeing Kyle in the Fall right around the time he started school. Unfortunately it was at a funeral. Kyle's grandfather had passed away suddenly, and the whole family was devastated. Kyle seemed to be particularly upset. Apparently he had been really close to his grandfather. Kyle loves baseball and his grandfather used to play semi-pro. Kyle was proud of all the trophies and plaques and old photos. During the service, Kyle was inconsolable, crying non-stop. I felt so bad for him. I know he missed a couple of days of school after that. Maybe that had something to do with what happened to him, I'm not sure. The absence put him behind the other kids in his class. I know he struggled to catch up but he'd already started off the year on the wrong foot. He was also having trouble adjusting to grade six. Half the class was full of new kids. And the homework load was heavier than he was used to. He began to get depressed.

"A month or so after the funeral Jack and Betty invited Trish and me over for dinner. I wondered how Kyle was doing. And when I saw him, I could tell he wasn't doing well. As we all greeted each other, I saw Kyle standing off by the stairs with his head down. I walked over and he gave me a weak little handshake. Normally he's excited to see me, giving me high-fives, punching me in the shoulder. He's your basic wiry eleven-year-old with a mop of messy blond hair. But tonight he looked skinnier than normal, and he had a sullen look on his face – like he hadn't smiled in weeks.

"At the dinner table he sat there listlessly. Betty and Jack had prepared a great meal – lasagna and caesar salad – and we all had second helpings, except for Kyle. He just pushed his food around on his plate, taking meagre nibbles every time his mom or dad glanced at him. Normally he's a pretty talkative kid, always yapping about baseball, who his favorite players are, who sucks. He's the kind of kid that knows all the stats, every player's batting average. But that night he was silent. When he did say something you could hardly hear him.

"After dinner, Kyle and his sister disappeared upstairs and we all had a chance to talk about Kyle. Betty and Jack were obviously concerned. It had been a month since the funeral and still Kyle seemed so down about everything. Betty told us that Kyle had been withdrawn ever since. Most days after school he'd just go straight up to his room. Some nights he wouldn't even come down for dinner. 'We tried getting him to come down and eat,' Betty said, 'but what was I supposed to do, send an army up there to get him. I want him to eat, but nothing seems to be working. Sometimes I get to the point where I'm practically crying outside his room. It's scary. I don't know what to do.'

"I didn't know what to say. I shrugged my shoulders and looked at Trish for help. But neither of us had had much experience with kids. Torin hadn't been born yet, and although I was already working closely with school kids as part of the street crime unit, I figured this thing with Kyle was over my head. I didn't really know what was normal behaviour for Kyle. I mean, his grandfather had passed away only a month ago. I just figured he'd come out of this mood eventually. Hopefully he'd be back to normal and smiling again in a few weeks. Unfortunately there was more to Kyle's condition than just his grandfather's death. But nobody knew what it was until too late. We ended the evening on a down note. Betty and Jack seemed worried about Kyle so Trish and I thought it best not to make it a late evening.

"We didn't hear from Betty and Jack again until about a month later when Betty called Trish one evening. She was frantic. In fact, I could hear her crying over the phone from the other side of the room. Trish did her best to calm her down and reassure her, but I could tell by Trish's face that it wasn't going well. After a few minutes of sympathetic listening, Trish told her we'd be right over and hung up. When she put down the phone I looked over at Trish, anxiously waiting to find out what had happened. Trish closed her eyes and told me that Kyle had been rushed to the hospital that afternoon with a badly broken nose. We both looked at each other shaking our heads. We knew exactly what each other was thinking – Kyle's injury was no accident. Betty hadn't told Trish that. In fact, at that point, Betty didn't even know herself.

"Trish and I drove out to the hospital and met Betty and Jack in the waiting area. Both of them were really shook up. Kyle was knocked out on anesthetics and the doctors were trying to set the bone. He'd be bandaged up for quite a while before anybody would be able to tell how it turned out. We never saw Kyle that night, but Betty had and she was practically in shock from the sight. Kyle's whole face was swollen. His eyes were black and puffed out and you could barely see his pupils.

"'How did it happen?' I asked.

"'I don't know,' Betty said. 'One of the kids at the school said he slipped while running and fell face-first on the pavement.'

"And that was all anybody knew for sure until a couple of days later when Kyle was conscious enough to tell his mother what really happened. The truth was a group of kids had swarmed Kyle outside the back of the school. They had circled around him, calling him names and taking shots at him. One of the kids had started punching him in the gut, and Kyle had fallen to the ground, holding onto his stomach. Then another kid had walked up and kicked him square in the face. That was probably the kick that had broken his nose, but the kid had kept kicking him, causing even more damage. They all scrambled away, I guess, when the blood started pouring from Kyle's face.

"Betty and Jack were alarmed. They had no idea Kyle went to a school where kids did things like that. They couldn't explain it. To them it was an absurd, random act of violence. However, as more details came out, the act, though utterly violent and cruel, did not appear to be random. One evening, a week or so after the beating, Betty came over to our house. Her face was drawn, her eyes blood-shot. She hadn't slept much in the past few days. She wanted to talk about Kyle's incident, wanted to understand how something like this could happen.

"I asked Betty if Kyle had said anything more about the kids that beat him up. In particular, I wanted to know if they'd been harassing him for a while before the final assault. Betty said she didn't know. I then asked her if she had noticed changes in Kyle other than his not eating and list-less behaviour. At first she told us she couldn't think of anything else, and then her eyes opened wide and she said, 'Well, you know, Kyle has missed his fair share of school days in the past few weeks.'

"'Was he sick?' I asked.

"'Well, I don't think so really. I just thought he was upset about his grandfather dying so I didn't make a big deal out of it. But that's something he's never done before.'

"'How about his grades. Do you know if his marks are slipping.'

"'Hmmm,' Betty said, 'you know, I'm not sure. Normally he comes to us and shows us his marks, you know, if he did well on a test or something, he'll let us know. But he hasn't done that this year.'

"'Well, Betty, I bet if you look a little closer, you'll probably find that Kyle's marks have slipped.' Betty shook her head sadly. I paused for a moment then continued, 'Betty, how about missing items?' I asked.

"'What do you mean?' Betty said.

"'I mean, have any of his belongings gone missing?'

"'Like what?' she asked.

"'A jacket. A Walkman. A bike, maybe. Anything like that?'

"Betty thought for a minute. 'Yes,' she said, 'you know, you're right. A couple of weeks ago I noticed Kyle wasn't walking around the house with his Walkman like he used to. You know, he's always got it on. Sometimes I think he was born with it wrapped around his head.' Betty managed a smile when she said that. And I saw her eyes grow wet. I thought about Kyle lying in his bed, half-asleep, with his face plastered with bandages. He should have been out playing ball hockey with the neighbourhood kids, or glued to his Sega Genesis like every other eleven-year-old. 'So,' Betty continued, 'when I didn't see him with his Walkman I asked him where it was. He kind of looked away and shrugged his shoulders. I asked him again, and he said he'd left it in his locker at school and ran upstairs. But I never saw him with his Walkman again. So, I guess you're right, he did have something go missing.'

"'Okay, Betty, what about injuries? I mean before his broken nose. Did he ever come home with any bruises and cuts or scrapes?'

"'I guess so. Once he came home with a bruise on his arm. One night I walked into the TV room and found him sleeping on the couch. I went to wake him up, you know, by shaking him a little. I had my hand on his arm, he was wearing a T-shirt and I saw, just under his sleeve, this dark area. I pushed it up a little and saw a giant bruise. It gave me a real start. I woke him up and asked him about it. He said he'd fallen during gym class. So I left it at that. Kids are always falling and hurting themselves, especially kids Kyle's age, so, you know, you don't think much about it.'

"We sat in silence for a moment or so after that, and then Betty asked, 'Kevin, are you saying these things are all connected?'

"'I think so, Betty. I think Kyle was having trouble with a group of kids for a while. His broken nose is only the culmination of it. They'd probably been picking on him for a while.'

"At that point Betty put her head in her hands and began to cry. Trish went over and sat beside her and put her arm around her. We were quiet for a while until Betty spoke up again. 'I feel terrible. It's my fault,' she said. 'I should have noticed. I should have known and done something about it. But I just sat around like an idiot while my son was coming home with bruises. He was getting picked on at school the whole time, and I did absolutely nothing.'

"'Betty, please, it's not your fault. You simply didn't know.'

"'How come he didn't tell me? I can't understand that at all. He kept it all inside. He must have been terrified. I can't imagine it – Kyle scared to go to school.'

"'Well,' I said, 'a lot of kids who get picked on at school don't go to their parents, or to any adult.'

"'But why?' Betty asked.

"'This is very important. Firstly, many kids think they will be called a rat if they report harassment or violence. No kid wants to be considered a rat by their friends. Kids are afraid of becoming social outcasts. Secondly, the kids that picked on him probably threatened him. You know, they probably said something like, 'If you tell anybody, we'll make it so you don't speak again.' That's usually the main reason kids keep to themselves – they're afraid. Some kids also don't tell anybody because they don't think their parents or their teachers can really do anything. They feel that they've got to solve it on their own.'

"'But why Kyle? He's such a good kid. Why would anybody want to beat him up?'

"'That's a good question,' I said, 'and one I've been thinking about. In Kyle's case, I think it had something to do with his grandfather passing away.'

"'How?' Betty asked.

"'Well, the kids that get picked on generally have one thing in common. They're unhappy. And that unhappiness may stem from a particular incident, like in Kyle's case, or it may stem from something in the kid's personality – low self-esteem, poor self-image, things like that. You see, kids at school can spot that in another kid right away. And instantly these kids are marked as victims. If there's a gang at the school, or a group of troublemakers, they'll want to take advantage of these unhappy kids. The troublemakers get their thrills from abusing kids like that. After the funeral, Kyle would have had trouble fitting in at school. While the other kids were busy socializing and making friends, Kyle was probably off on his own, sitting by himself. And the fact that he missed a few days of school right at the beginning of the year would only have added to his sense of not belonging. School would have seemed strange to him, and other kids would have viewed him right away as an outsider.'

"Betty grew quiet after that. I knew she still felt guilty. Trish and I reassured her that she did what anyone else would have done, but that didn't seem to relieve her much. She left us that night with a heavy weight on her shoulders. Fortunately Kyle's injury healed well. There's a slight bump on his nose now, but he's actually kind of proud of it because it reminds him of his grandfather who broke his own nose playing baseball back in the '30s. And he's not getting picked on anymore, thankfully. The two kids most responsible for his beating were eventually suspended. . . . Well," I said looking around at the parents in the classroom, "that's the end of my story. When we return, we'll see how you can help prevent your child from ending up a victim like Kyle."

9

WHAT YOU CAN DO AT HOME TO PROTECT YOUR KIDS

During the break I sat with Ian and Wendy at the back of the class. Wendy shook her head, "I can only imagine what nightmares Betty had about what happened to Kyle. You try your best to do the right thing for your kids, but sometimes it doesn't seem to be enough. I hope she's still not holding herself responsible?"

"No, I think she's over that now. Thankfully Kyle's not suffering any long-term effects. Everybody's managed to put it behind them. And some good did actually come out of it. Kyle and his parents are much closer. Kyle's not keeping things to himself like before. They spend a lot of time talking, hashing things out."

THE 19 WARNING SIGNS

One of the first questions came from Jackie. "Kevin," she said, "I found that story about Kyle scary. I mean, his grandfather had just died, so of course he's going to go into some kind of funk. How was Betty supposed to know that there was more to his change of mood than that?"

"Good question. And the short answer is knowledge. If Betty knew what the signs of being a victim were, she would have recognized them in her own son. But she didn't know, so even though the signs were there she couldn't see them." At that point Robert huffed. I looked over and saw him shake his head.

MISSING ITEMS AND MYSTERIOUS INJURIES

"Come on," Robert said, "if the signs were obvious why didn't you notice them when you were at Betty's and Jack's?"

"Well, unfortunately the tell-tale signs didn't come out till later and I didn't know about them until it was too late."

"Which signs were those?" Jackie asked.

"The two that really stick out are the missing Walkman and the bruise on the arm. Anytime a kid loses stuff like a Walkman, or a bike, I think it's wise to be suspicious. If they just shrug and tell you they lost it, I think you should look a little deeper. Bikes, Walkmans, jackets – these are the kinds of things that get stolen everyday. And the kids that steal them often steal them right off the person who owns them. Keep in mind our first most important point to understand about youth violence – 'Our kids are growing up in a radically different world.' Back when we were in school, the bad kids would rip off your locker when you weren't looking, but nowadays, they threaten their victims right out in the open and just take the stuff right then and there. It's a way of asserting power.

"I also strongly advise getting to the bottom of any injury. Don't let your kids just shrug them off. Remember, lots of kids are too scared to tell us the truth about what's happening. They're afraid that if they report it they'll just get harassed even more. Missing items and mysterious injuries are the really key signs that your child could be in trouble.

SKIPPING SCHOOL AND FALLING GRADES

"There are other signs to keep your eyes open for, such as skipping school and falling grades. Both of these could mean that your son or daughter is afraid of something at school. Perhaps they've had a bad run-in with a group of troublemakers and are now having trouble concentrating on school.

NOT EATING, NOT TALKING, BEING SECRETIVE, HAVING TROUBLE SLEEPING, UNHAPPINESS

"And there are other more subtle signs. Such as not eating, not talking much or being secretive, and having trouble sleeping. These, of course, are all indicators of depression. And certainly there are many reasons why a child might be depressed. Just because your child is unhappy doesn't mean that he or she is getting harassed or abused at school. However, it's important to remember that unhappy kids are the very kids that are likely to get picked on. Other kids at school are always on the lookout for vulnerable kids. So, if your kid seems depressed at home, there's a chance that some of his peers at school have their eye on him."

TALKING BACK AND A LACK OF RESPECT FOR AUTHORITY

Jackie spoke up, "In other words, Kevin, what you're saying is that if your kid is unhappy he's a sitting duck."

"Well, I guess that puts it bluntly," I said. "Sometimes, a victim will react in the opposite way. Instead of being silent and depressed, they become angry and lash out at those around them. Victims feel helpless and often they will strike out at a parent, friend or even a teacher because they lack any other outlet for their rage and fear. In this case, talking back or defying authority is an act of rebellion.

TATTOOS, INSIGNIA AND WILD CLOTHING

"That rage or frustration might also be expressed in other acts of rebellion, such as getting a tattoo or a body part pierced. Some kids will dress more wildly just to provoke their parents. Some even start wearing gang colours.

"Since we've come up with a fair number of warning signs," I said, "I think it would be helpful to capture them on the blackboard." I wrote up the warning signs we had covered so far.

"Are there any other signs we should watch out for – signs that you know about from other experiences that weren't evident in Kyle's situation?" Wendy asked.

LOW SELF-ESTEEM

"Yes. I think we should add low self-esteem to our list."

"Do you think there's a big difference between unhappiness and low self-esteem?" Jackie asked.

"I'm not a psychologist. But for our purposes, I guess the Kyle example comes in handy. I wouldn't say that Kyle had low self-esteem, but I would say that he was very unhappy. I think of unhappiness as a general term, and low self-esteem as something specific. Low self-esteem is part of a kid's personality; it's something ingrained. Whereas, some forms of unhappiness, like Kyle's, are temporary. Kyle was unhappy because he was a healthy kid reacting to a real situation. It was only a matter of time before he was back on his feet again, but a lot of the kids I see who end up being victims are kids with low self-esteem – kids who don't have a healthy image of themselves. They're easily influenced by the bad kids. They are more easily frightened and more likely to keep things to themselves. . . . So, let's add low self-esteem to our list."

"Any others, Kevin?" Wendy asked.

A LACK OF FRIENDS, FRIENDS YOU DON'T KNOW, OR TROUBLEMAKING FRIENDS

"There's a few more I'd like to add. A good sign to watch out for is the company your kids are keeping. It's important to make sure you know who their friends are because we know that kids who hang out with troublemakers end up victims more often than kids with a solid group of decent friends. A lack of friends could also be a bad sign. It could mean your child has trouble socializing at school. And if they're lonely, they're probably unhappy and if they're unhappy. . . . well, we know what that can lead to." I turned to the blackboard again and wrote up these last two points.

AWAY FROM HOME A LOT

"Okay," I said, "I have one other point to add to the list – is your child away from home a lot? Kids who stay out late hanging around downtown, at the arcades, or at the local mall are more likely to report being victimized than kids who stay home. In fact, this was confirmed by that study of students done in Calgary I referred to before the holidays. I suppose there are various reasons for this. Kids who don't like staying home are probably not very happy with their lives. They're looking for fun and excitement and support elsewhere. This kind of neediness makes them vulnerable. And when bad kids spot this vulnerability, they're going to exploit it. Also, kids who are out a lot are exposed to bad kids more often – and this increases their chances of becoming a victim. They're not going to get beat up if they're at home reading or watching TV or playing table tennis with their brothers and sisters and parents. . . . I'm not saying we have to imprison our kids at home, but I do think we have to make sure things aren't taken to the extreme. If your kid is out seven nights a week, you should probably be asking yourself why."

I scribbled this last point on the blackboard and then numbered the entire list. "Well," I said turning around, "that makes 19. This is just a partial list of the warning signs you should look for, but it should be helpful. Just remember that all kids are individuals and will react differently if they are harassed, threatened or assaulted. I think we developed a fairly helpful list, so why don't we leave it there."

13 THINGS YOU CAN DO AT HOME TO PROTECT YOUR KIDS

A silence hung in the room. I could sense a feeling of worry. All the parents were probably thinking about their own children and wondering if they have ever showed any of the warning signs. I wanted to make sure all the parents here tonight understood that there are things we can do. "Okay," I said, "I think it's time we turned our discussion towards finding solutions. Let's take Kyle's story and this list of warning signs as a starting point for a list of things we can do to stop our kids from becoming victims. And as we talk, I'm going to capture our points on the blackboard."

I saw a few heads nod and then turned to the blackboard and wrote 'Things you can do at home to protect your kids.' "So," I said, "any ideas? And remember, we should phrase them as actions – things we can do right away when we go home."

SOLUTION 1: LOOK FOR THE WARNING SIGNS OF VICTIMIZATION AND REACT

Wendy spoke up, "Look for the warning signs of victimization and react."

"Okay," I said, writing down her point. "A good way to understand the signs we discussed is to think about them in terms of the Violence Ladder. The signs in the Kyle story were all symptoms of the Violence Ladder. As a victim, Kyle was harassed, threatened, had things stolen, was roughed up by a group of kids and ultimately seriously beaten. And along the way, the signs told the story – only no one was watching. We have to learn to recognize the signs of victimization and then break the Violence Ladder.

"Any other points from Kyle's story?" I asked.

SOLUTION 2: MAKE SURE YOUR KIDS ARE HAPPY

Jackie broke the silence and exclaimed, "Make sure your kids are happy."

Everyone seemed to murmur in agreement.

"Good. Simple, but true," I said as I wrote down Jackie's point.

"You know," Jackie said, "it's hard sometimes, but with my son Edwin, I remember playing a lot more with him when he was my only child. It used to make me so sad to see him upset. I would make faces and tickle him just to get him to smile. But now that I have another child, I'm just not putting that same amount of energy into taking care of Edwin. I don't want to spoil him, and giving him time to sort things out on his own is good, but I think I should pay more attention to him when it's clear something is bothering him. You know, sometimes it might be something small that is making him upset, and it's better to deal with that right away than letting it really get him down. Anyway, I never thought about happiness in terms of protecting your child, but I can see how important it is now."

WHAT YOU NEED TO KNOW FOR SOLUTIONS 3 - 9

WHY KIDS DON'T TALK

"I think now would be a good time to go back to one of our stories from last year," I said. "In fact, if you can remember, it was the first story I told you way back in September – the story about Jamie and Rick. Jamie was the kid who got picked on by Rick and his gang. Rick wanted to sell Jamie a knife but Jamie refused to buy it. That started a nasty escalation of violence that went on for days. And Jamie never told a soul about being harassed. His parents got involved only when someone who saw the gang assault Jamie called 911. When we discussed this story we realized how important it is to tell our children to talk to us, to tell us when someone at school is giving them a hard time. I think tonight we should take that a step further. I don't think it's enough just to tell our kids to report things. There are reasons our kids don't talk to us, and unless we deal with those reasons head on, there will always be a barrier of silence between us and our kids. . . . Can anyone remember the reasons why Jamie didn't go to his parents for help until it was too late?"

KIDS ARE AFRAID OF RETALIATION

Lydia, who'd been quiet up until now, spoke up. "He was afraid," she said.

"Of what?" I asked.

"Of the bullies," she answered. "I guess he was scared they'd hurt him even more."

"How real is that fear?" Wendy asked. "Do bullies go after someone who finks on them? I wouldn't want a gang of kids with a vendetta after one of my boys."

"Yeah," Jackie said, "what does happen? Are students being beaten up for ratting? Are they in danger?"

"Be careful not to call it ratting," I said. "Parents must make sure that kids understand the clear and distinct difference between being a tattle-tale and reporting a violent act. Also, your kids should know that you're not asking them to do something you wouldn't do. A parent who was assaulted would not go and form their own gang; they would call the police – and our children should as well.

"As for retaliation, I've been doing this job for almost ten years, and I can say confidently that retaliation is just not an issue. I was surprised at first, because intuitively you'd think that offenders would strike back. Remember, there are only a few really bad apples, and these kids – the serious offenders – get their power from being able to rally a gang behind them. Once the school and police are involved and steps are taken to deal with the offender, the other kids, the followers, get scared. Without their leader, they're usually totally harmless. And when they see that there are serious consequences to their actions and that the school, parents and police won't tolerate what they're doing, then they are highly unlikely to take a shot at a kid who they suspect will report something. The child is sending a clear message that they have a responsible and mature attitude. Plus, in programs like Student Crime Stoppers, which we will be talking about in another meeting, the student who is leaving us the information is always guaranteed their anonymity.

"Remember, a bully doesn't usually just pick on one person. So, it's important to tell our kids that if they do report a bully to you or the school or the police, they will become a positive influence on those other good kids.

"Recently I was at a local school, showing 500 grade 7 and 8 students my 'Tackle Violence' video and talking about this issue. While I was packing up my stuff after the lecture I was approached by a grade-8 girl named Jill and what she told me really crystallized my thoughts on bullies, retaliation and revenge.

"She told me that when she had been in grade 7, she used to have to pick up her 9-year-old brother from the local grade school and walk home with him. They took the same route every night because a river cut across their route and there was only one bridge crossing it. One day, an older kid that they didn't recognize was hanging around on the bridge and, as they tried to pass, he stepped in front of them to block their way. Jill grabbed her brother's hand and tried to squeeze past the stranger, hoping that he'd leave them alone. Instead, as she stepped beside him, he grabbed her shoulder and whirled her around. Before she could react, he punched her squarely in the face. As she covered her nose with her hands and screamed, her little brother threw himself at the bigger kid, but he was far too small to help. The bully easily pushed him to the ground and then started kicking him in the shins.

"When they got home that night, Jill's mother gasped when she noticed the huge bruise on her son's shin. When she asked what had happened, Jill lied to her and said that her brother had hurt himself playing soccer. Jill's nose was a little bruised as well but her mother didn't notice and Jill hoped that was the end of the matter. Unfortunately, the same bully was waiting for them at the bridge again the next night, and for many nights after that.

"Quietly, Jill and her brother suffered the assaults. She couldn't concentrate in class, because all day long she worried about crossing that bridge, and at night she was so worried she couldn't sleep. Eventually the stress made her physically ill. After a month she finally burst into tears at the dinner table and confessed everything to her mother and father.

"In Jill's own words, her mother immediately did 'the worst thing' she could have done – she called the police. And, according to Jill, the police did the worst thing they could have done – they arrested the bully. She was so scared of this guy that she would have rather put up with a small beating everyday than have someone confront him and potentially make the situation worse. When she heard that the police charged him with assault, she thought he would find her and kill her.

"She told me that, the next day, she was constantly looking over her shoulder as she walked around the school. Between classes she even went down different stairwells than she normally did to try and avoid him. But, that night, when Jill and her brother got to the bridge, the bully wasn't there. As she said, 'The last day he ever touched me was the day I reported him.'

"What that story made me realize was that bullies always expect two things to happen whenever they pick on a victim. Number one, they assume that their victim will be too afraid to say anything to anybody. And, if this is the case, it means that they will have a ready-made victim available everyday. Number two, they think that if the victim has any reaction at all, it would be to form a gang of their own for self-defence, as we saw in the case of Kathy and Lenore. Forming a new gang plays right into the hands of the bully, because they are battle-hardened and would probably win a straight fight.

"However, if the victim does not do either of these things, and, instead, reports the incident, the offender will be neutralized. Bullies don't have a coping mechanism for dealing with a kid who speaks up and, for the most part, bullies certainly don't want to face court and jail time. It's just common sense."

Both Wendy and Jackie sighed noticeably and the other parents seemed to appreciate the reassurance.

"So," I asked, "can anyone think of other reasons why Jamie was afraid?"

KIDS ARE AFRAID NO ONE WILL TAKE THEM SERIOUSLY

"He was afraid no one would take him seriously," Robert shouted out.

"How could someone not take him seriously?" Lydia asked, perplexed. "If my son Joey came to me and said he was in trouble, I'd be worried sick. I'd want to know exactly what was going on and I'd make sure something was done."

"Well," Robert said, "it's like Kevin says, things have changed since we went to school. Last year, my oldest son, Todd, mentioned to me that some kid at school was giving him a hard time. I took him out back and taught him how to throw a punch. I don't know how he actually handled it because I never heard about it again. Knowing what I know now, I guess he figured I had no idea what he was going through. I realize what I did was pretty stupid – some of these kids are running around in gangs and carrying weapons. But at the time, I guess I thought it was just something minor. That's what my dad did with me – taught me how to defend myself."

"– that's terrifying," Lydia exclaimed. "What if your son throws a punch at some kid and then gets stabbed."

"I know," Robert said defensively. "I've spoken to Todd since. I've told him to just come to me next time, or to talk to the principal, or his teacher. He's not the fighting type anyway – which is a good thing, I guess."

"That's good," I said. "And, another point to add is that we must be careful not to send mixed messages to our children. Kids get confused when parents tell them to defend themselves, the police tell them to report all violent incidents, and TV and movies glorify violence as a way of solving problems.

KIDS ARE AFRAID THEIR PARENTS WILL GET ANGRY

"Can you think of any other reasons why kids might be afraid to tell us what's going on?" I asked. "I'm thinking of something in particular from the Kyle story," I said.

I saw a few heads shake.

"How about his stolen Walkman?" I said.

"Why would that make him afraid?" Lydia asked.

"I can see what Kevin means," Wendy said. "Put yourself in Kyle's shoes. Maybe that Walkman was a gift, or maybe it was really expensive and his parents kept telling him to make sure he takes care of it. I know I do that with expensive stuff. You know how kids are – they don't really appreciate their belongings. So maybe Kyle was afraid his parents would give him heck if they found out he'd lost it. You know, some parents might think he just wasn't taking care of his stuff. And even if his parents wouldn't have reacted like that, it's enough that Kyle thought they would."

"And same goes for the injury too," Robert said gruffly. "I'm always playing the tough father – I want my kids to be able to take care of themselves. I can see how Todd wouldn't want me to see him bruised up. He'd probably think I'd think he was a wimp. And last year, that's maybe how I would have reacted."

"I guess the point here is to realize that kids sometimes have a screwed-up way of looking at things," Ian said. "Their reasons for not talking might be absurd to us, but to them it makes perfect sense – many children just aren't mature enough to do the right thing. I know I had crazy ideas when I was a kid. We used to live close to the school. It was a three-minute walk. But I'd go an extra four blocks out of my way to walk home from school. It would take me ten minutes, but I did it because one of the older kids that lived next door told me that the German shepherd down the street was really a wolf that ate little kids. I was petrified – and stupid, I guess."

"Okay," I said, "I'm sure there are other reasons why kids don't report things."

KIDS DON'T KNOW WHO TO GO TO

"Maybe they don't know who to go to," Wendy suggested.

"I think that's true in some cases," I said. "They don't know who to go to because they don't know who can help. To use Robert's story as an example, his son Todd effectively wrote his dad off. No offense, Robert, but your son realized that you weren't much help. Maybe he felt the same about his teachers or the school principal. He probably felt like he was on his own. Consider that kids always go to each other first, long before they go to their parents. And the most disastrous thing a kid can do when faced with a bully is to go to his friends, rather than an authority. With his friends behind him, he may win the day, but the battle has just begun – the bully will gather his own gang and retaliate.

KIDS FEEL THEY ARE ON THEIR OWN

"In fact," I said, "a lot of kids feel that they are on their own. As parents, we want our kids to be independent, to take care of themselves, but we also want them to know when they're in over their heads and when to come to us for help. This is an important point because kids today are dealing with heavy issues at an early age. Today, your basic twelve-year-old knows quite a bit about drugs, sex and violence. When I was twelve I knew quite a bit about *The Brady Bunch*, snow cones and baseball. Today, kids feel an immense pressure to grow up fast. They are bombarded with ads promoting awareness about AIDS, drugs, sex and condoms. The media plays a big role in our children's lives and sometimes we are so busy that our kids feel that they shouldn't bother us with minor problems. They feel that their problems are small when compared to the giant media issues they are confronted with all day long.

KIDS DON'T WANT TO BECOME OUTCASTS

"On top of just feeling that they're on their own, kids are terrified of actually being deserted by their friends. They feel that their friends are the most important people in the world. They're afraid they might lose their friends or become a social outcast if they report a case of harassment or violence. In fact, they may become outcasts temporarily, but their true friends would admire their courage to do the right thing.

KIDS MIGHT NOT KNOW WHEN THINGS GET SERIOUS

"I'd like to add another reason why kids don't report harassment. We've talked a great deal about the Violence Ladder. In hindsight, we know that Kyle's broken nose was the end result of a long series of incidents. And that first incident may have been a wrong look, or a name calling. In fact, the majority of violence has a meaningless beginning, as was the case in Lenore's story. She thought that Kathy was stealing her boyfriend, but they were just discussing a test. When the media reports violent crime, people often assume the causes were drug or gang related. But in most cases, the root causes are things like a rumour, a case of mistaken identity, or a stolen item – like shoes or a Walkman.

"Do you think Kyle was aware that that first insignificant run-in was going to lead to a serious injury? Kyle may not have known exactly when things got really dangerous. Kids don't report to their teachers that so-and-so gave them a bad stare, or bumped into them in the hallway. How could they prove it. And who'd take them seriously. Also, the intimidation might be so subtle that the victim himself is not even aware there's serious tension building. You know, part of him is thinking he's just being paranoid – 'Am I being followed or not?'

"Let's recap the list of reasons why kids don't talk and then develop solutions that will make sure our kids do talk. Okay, we said they're afraid of retaliation, they're afraid no one will take them seriously, and they're afraid their parents will be angry. We also said that they don't know who to go to, that they feel they are on their own, that they don't want to become outcasts, and that they might not know when things get serious – I believe I got them all." I stepped over to our list on the blackboard and held the piece of chalk in the air ready to write down another solution. "Solutions anybody?" I asked.

"Yeah," Robert said, "take every point you just listed and phrase it as an action."

"What do you mean?" Lydia asked.

SOLUTION 3: TELL YOUR KIDS NOT TO BE
AFRAID OF RETALIATION

"Kevin says that the kids are afraid of retaliation. So, our solution is 'Tell your kids not to be afraid of retaliation,'" Robert said. "If the kids have nothing to fear about reporting incidents, they should know that. If I was them, I'd want the same assurance. I'd want to know that I wasn't putting myself in jeopardy by going to the principal and saying that so-and-so threatened me in the hall."

"Good," I said writing down Robert's suggestion. "So we should tell our kids that there is much less risk in going to a principal than doing nothing, and possibly getting hurt, or getting a gang together and retaliating."

"You want to continue, Robert?" I asked.

SOLUTION 4: SHOW YOUR KIDS YOU UNDERSTAND THEIR WORLD

"Sure," he said. "Next, if the kids are worried we won't take them seriously we have to assure them that we will. In other words, we have to let them know that we appreciate what they're going through. The key to understanding their world is getting all the information you can from your child's school, the police and other organizations in your community. We need to be well-informed and show our children that we understand their world, and we have to stop applying all our outdated notions of what it's like to be in school. Like I said before, if my son comes to me and says some kid at school is picking on him, I'm not going to tell him to go beat him up like I did before. I'm going to take it seriously. I'm going to want him to tell me what's going on, and then I'm going to take it up with the school. And I'm going to make sure that my son feels safe about going to school."

"I'll capture that as 'Show your kids you understand their world,'" I said, and wrote it on the blackboard.

SOLUTION 5: SHOW YOUR KIDS THAT YOUR FIRST
CONCERN IS FOR THEIR SAFETY

"Next," Robert said, "is to assure them we won't get angry. They have to know that our first concern is for their safety. We have to show them that we don't care about their expensive clothes or their Walkmans. It's their physical and mental health that matters. If we find out that their

Walkman got stolen, we shouldn't launch into a speech about how expensive it was, and how money doesn't grow on trees, and how they don't take care of anything because they didn't buy it with their own money. Instead, we should try to find out exactly what happened, and see if there is a bigger problem lurking beneath it all – you know, see if they are getting harassed at school. That way, they'll know we are worried about them, not the Walkman."

"Okay," I said, "I'm going to write 'Show your kids that your first concern is for their safety.'"

SOLUTION 6: SHOW YOUR KIDS YOU CAN PROTECT THEM

Robert continued, "Then there's the point that they don't know who to go to because they don't think we can help. So, our solution is to show them we will protect them. We have to establish their confidence in us as protectors. And I guess that goes for the schools and police as well."

"Yes," I said, "if our kids believe that their teachers, the police, and their parents know how to handle the situation they will go to them for help. It's when they doubt our abilities that they stop coming to us. We'll go into the specifics about how a concerted effort between the police, the schools and parents can protect our kids in another session, so, tonight, I'll write down 'Show your kids you can protect them.'"

SOLUTION 7: SHOW YOUR KIDS THEY ARE NOT ALONE

Wendy spoke up at this point. "As far as our kids feeling they are on their own, I think we have to show them that they are not alone. They should know that we don't expect them to handle everything by themselves. They're still children, you know. I guess there's a fine line between wanting them to be independent and wanting them to know when to come to us. Like Jackie said, you want your kids to learn how to solve problems. But if the issue has anything to do with their safety, we certainly don't want them handling it on their own. In this case, I guess actions speak louder than words. We had neighbours, for instance, whose son, Lorne, had the bike he rides to school spray-painted by some students from another school. The kids who did it were from one of the basketball teams that compete against the team Lorne plays on. Anyway, when he told his parents, they told him to report it to the principal, but he didn't. He was too scared. His parents, I guess, figured he was adult enough to deal with it on his own. But they were wrong. He didn't go to anybody, and then a couple of weeks later, after another game, his locker was destroyed and stuff was stolen – his watch, and a bunch of CDs. His parents went to see the school about it then, but they should have gone to the principal after the first incident. They should have gone with Lorne. And all of them – Lorne, his parents, and the principal – should have discussed how to deal with the issue. That way, Lorne would have known that he wasn't alone."

I wrote down 'Show your kids they are not alone.'

SOLUTION 8: TEACH YOUR KIDS TO BE INDIVIDUALS

I turned to face the parents and said, "Also, don't forget that kids don't want to become outcasts. They need to know that being an individual and acting responsibly will not mean being an outcast, because true friends will support them when they make tough decisions. We must coach our children; teach them to look out for themselves and make smart choices. This is such an important point that we will discuss it again next month. I don't think we can emphasize it enough."

I wrote down 'Teach your kids to be individuals.'

SOLUTION 9: TEACH YOUR KIDS ABOUT THE VIOLENCE LADDER

"Don't forget the last reason why kids don't talk," said Wendy. "The fact that kids might not realize that harassment has the potential to become serious needs to be dealt with. I think our children need to know how violence escalates. We should tell them about the Violence Ladder – they should know how relatively insignificant things can lead to serious violence. If Jamie from your first story last year knew that he was in trouble as soon as Rick started pressuring him about buying the knife, I think he would have realized he should speak to somebody about it. He should have been able to recognize what was going on as the first step on the Violence Ladder. As soon as kids start getting harassed or threatened they should know that something serious is going on."

As Wendy was talking I scribbled on the black board 'Teach your kids about the Violence Ladder.'

SOLUTION 10: MAKE SURE YOU GET THE COMPLETE STORY

I stood back and scanned our list. We had just added another seven solutions. "Well," I said, "we've devoted seven separate solutions to trying to get our kids to talk to us. That's a lot, but I think it's necessary — a lack of communication is one of the biggest reasons violence continues to permeate our schools and communities."

"Kevin," Wendy said, "what if you follow those solutions and still your kid isn't talking to you?"

"Well, good question," I said. "In that case, I think it's important to be persistent. As parents, we must do everything we can to get at the truth. If your kid comes home and you notice something suspicious, you have to ask them what the problem is, but don't stop when they simply shrug and run up the stairs. I'm not saying we should be paranoid nervous wrecks. We don't want to send the message to our kids that we're out of control. We have to be calm, but persistent. A technique that we as police officers use is to continue to ask the same question. You'll find that every time you ask the question you'll get more information. Also, another technique is to watch your child's body language. If his eyes dart to his dominant side – the right-side for right-handed people, left for left-handed people – instead of looking at you when answering your question, then he's probably not telling you the truth. Once you spot a weakness in a kid's story, they are pretty easy to crack. . . . So, I think I should capture these ideas under a new solution." I wrote down the following: 'Make sure you get the complete story.'

SOLUTION 11: ALWAYS BE IMPROVING YOUR CHILD'S SELF-ESTEEM

Lydia spoke up at this point. "Kevin," she said, "I think we should add a couple more solutions based on the list of signs we developed. I think self-esteem is a big enough issue that it justifies its own solution. If kids with low self-esteem are the ones getting picked on, then we should make sure our kids have high self-esteem. How about phrasing it as 'Always be improving your child's self-esteem.'"

"I agree," said Wendy. "I think that's something we all do naturally, but I'm sure we all miss opportunities. I can think of one that happened to me the other day. My fourteen-year-old, Alex, is kind of a video-game junkie – not to the extent that he doesn't get his homework done, but he does play a lot, almost every night, I think. Anyway, he plays this one game over and over again and I think he's pretty good at it. The other night I heard him shouting from the den where he plays. Then he came running up the stairs and into the living room where I was reading. He was panting and all excited. He wanted to tell me how he just got his highest score. He was beaming. But I just raised my eyebrows and muttered, 'That's good,' then asked him if he'd finished his homework. Immediately his face fell and he shuffled off downstairs. I think he played for another two hours in total silence while I stewed upstairs. You see, it wasn't that I wasn't excited for him. How could I not be, it obviously made him so happy. But I guess I didn't want to encourage what I consider to be a waste of his time. . . . But you know, I've read that these video games aren't that bad. They say they help improve concentration and coordination and they get kids used to computers – stuff that will be important when he hits the work force. And I guess if he wasn't playing video games he'd probably being staring at the TV. So, in hindsight, I think I should have told him that I was proud and showed him that I was genuinely happy."

"I think that's a great example of how to improve your child's self-esteem in a small way," I said. "And, as we'll see next month, self-esteem is a very important issue when it comes to youth violence – not just for protecting victims, but also for preventing youth offenders in the first place."

SOLUTION 12: GET INVOLVED WITH YOUR KIDS

"Another solution we can draw from the list of warning signs," Lydia said, "is based on the one about your kids staying out a lot. I think the solution is to make sure you do stuff as a family. You know, it's difficult when you're so busy. Sometimes you really appreciate the break when your kids are out. The house is so quiet. But I think we really have to make the effort to do things they enjoy. Being together as a family has to be fun for them, otherwise they'll just look for their entertainment outside the house. Like Wendy, my kids play a lot of video games. A few months ago, my son Pino was showing me one of his games. I can't remember what it was. They all look the same to me. Anyway, he wanted me to play with him, but I said no. I didn't even try. I guess I felt intimidated, or something. But he seemed a little upset. And now I regret it. I should have at least tried. He probably would have enjoyed teaching me something, or at least beating me. And you know, he's started going out to the arcades now. Maybe if we'd gotten more involved. . . . The kids would probably appreciate it."

"Well, the truth is, if your kids are at home with you having fun, they're not going to get into any trouble," I said. "Okay, so I'll put that up as another solution – 'Get involved with your kids.'"

SOLUTION 13: ENCOURAGE YOUR CHILD TO PARTICIPATE IN EXTRACURRICULAR ACTIVITIES

"Kevin," Lydia said, "I have another solution related to these two ideas. I think a great way of raising your child's self-esteem and getting the whole family involved is to encourage your kids to get involved in school sports or the music program. You know, something where they can accomplish things. And the whole family should go see some of the games or go to the recitals. I'm sure we all do that, but I guess we don't realize that all this can ultimately have an impact on our child's safety."

"Good idea," I said. "I'll write that down as 'Encourage your child to participate in extracurricular activities.'"

SUMMARY

I stood back and looked at our list – thirteen great solutions. "Well," I said, "that's a fairly complete list, and we have run pretty late tonight, but I think it was time well-spent."

THE 19 WARNING SIGNS

1. Missing items
2. Mysterious injuries
3. Skipping school
4. Falling grades
5. Not eating
6. Not talking
7. Being secretive
8. Having trouble sleeping
9. Unhappiness
10. Talking back
11. Lack of respect for authority
12. Tattoos
13. Insignia
14. Wild clothing
15. Low self-esteem
16. Lack of friends
17. Friends you don't know
18. Troublemaking friends
19. Away from home a lot

13 THINGS YOU CAN DO AT HOME TO PROTECT YOUR KIDS

1. Look for the warning signs of victimization and react

2. Make sure your kids are happy

3. Tell your kids not to be afraid of retaliation

4. Show your kids you understand their world

5. Show your kids that your first concern is for their safety

6. Show your kids you can protect them

7. Show your kids they are not alone

8. Teach your kids to be individuals

9. Teach your kids about the Violence Ladder

10. Make sure you get the complete story

11. Always be improving your child's self-esteem

12. Get involved with your kids

13. Encourage your child to participate in extracurricular activities

10

No More Offenders

Just before the start of our February meeting, Robert came up to the front of the room to say hello.

"How are the kids?" I asked.

"Oh, good," he replied. "They're both looking forward to the summer. Danny is finishing grade 2 and Todd will be graduating from grade 8. I think he's actually a little nervous about going into high school next year."

"No more problems with bullies or anything?" I asked. "I remember you told us that Todd had been having a hard time last year. Some of the other kids were picking on him. . . ."

"No, everything's fine now. And, I guess, most importantly, they both know that if they're bullied or harassed they should come to me or tell one of their teachers. I'm reformed now. Since I've been coming to these meetings I've changed my position on fighting," he said a little sheepishly.

"Good, good. You don't want your kid to be a wimp, but you don't want him to be seriously injured either. And that's a real possibility as you've heard."

"Yeah, I guess the problem's really with me. It's just the way I am. I've never backed down from a confrontation and I didn't think my son should either. But now I see what problems that can cause. I guess I've mellowed with age," Robert said, then moved to take his seat.

"Okay, everyone," I said, "I think this is one of our most important sessions.

"If you remember, our last meeting focused on protecting our children from youth violence by preventing them from becoming victims.

122

We came up with 19 signs to warn us if our children have become victims and, also, 13 strategies to prevent them from ever becoming victims. But that's still not enough. Unfortunately, no matter how well we take care of our own child there will always be offenders out there.

"In fact, the only way to protect our kids for certain is to make sure there are no offenders. We must completely break the Violence Ladder. So, tonight I'd like to spend some time coming up with ways to do this. And when I talk about eliminating offenders I'm not talking about reacting to their crimes and arresting them. I'm talking about preventing their offending behaviour in the first place. This means, of course, that parents like us need to become more involved outside of the home. We need to get involved in the schools and in our communities. Ultimately, if we could take what we're learning here and put it into action across the rest of the country, we would go a long way toward eliminating youth violence.

"Tonight's story will help launch us on this topic. I'd like you to pay particular attention to the father because this is actually a story about how not to deal with young offenders. I think it is important for us to get involved, and I want to stress this, but I think we really have to know when and how to get involved. The following case was one that I worked on about a year ago and it shows you what happens when things go wrong.

George's story

"George and his wife Louise had bought their 11-year-old son, Brad, a mountain bike for his birthday in September. And, of course, Brad rode it everywhere – over to his friends, to school, even in the rain. He loved it. One Saturday, a few weeks after he'd bought Brad his bike, George sent Brad to the store on the corner for a few things.

"Outside the store, Brad leaned his bike against the plate glass window. He couldn't see a secure pole nearby, so he took his lock from around the seat post and locked his front wheel to the frame and ran inside – making sure that he could see his bike at all times while he was inside the store. He was still nervous though – a few kids at school had recently had their bikes stolen. As he ran around the aisles, grabbing the items on his list, he glanced outside at his bike balanced against the glass. It seemed to take forever for the guy ahead of him to pay for his merchandise. Brad told me he was sweating about his bike standing unattended outside. As soon as he got to the counter, he threw his money down, grabbed the change and then took off outside. The bike was still there, unharmed.

"As he was unlocking the wheel and frame, Brad suddenly heard several sets of footsteps and then another kid's voice. 'Nice bike,' the kid behind him said, sarcastically. Straightening up, Brad turned and saw four older boys standing in front of him. The closest one to him, standing a little bit ahead of the others, had long, stringy brown hair, ripped jeans and a jean jacket. Brad definitely hadn't seen them around before. Suddenly he became very scared.

"'I said, nice bike,' the kid said again. There was a lump in Brad's throat. He had the lock in his hands and his bike was standing right beside him. Brad thought that if he ditched the bag of groceries he had under his arm, he might be able to jump on his bike and get away if he needed to. But, as he told me, he certainly wasn't sure about that; these kids were a lot bigger and a lot older than him.

"Instead of running away, Brad stammered, 'Yeah, yeah. Thanks. I uh, just got it.' He turned slowly to throw his leg over the seat, hoping to ride away calmly. Behind him, the kids all laughed. Suddenly, the first kid grabbed his arm. Brad screamed. The groceries tumbled from his arms and his bike fell to the pavement. The older kid dragged Brad away from the store window, leaving his bike lying on the sidewalk. 'Shut up you little suck. We're taking the bike,' he said and then pushed Brad, who was crying and trembling, into the doorway of the closed antique shop beside the corner store.

"All of the kids were laughing and one of them, looking around to make sure that nobody was watching, picked up the bike while another one pulled a chocolate bar from the plastic bag on the sidewalk. The kid who was leading the group – his name turned out to be Nelson – said to Brad, 'If you tell anyone about this, I'll find you and kill you, you little puke. I know where you live and I know where you go to school.'

"Slowly Nelson turned and started to walk away, the other kids following him, one of them wheeling the bike. As they reached the edge of the sidewalk, Nelson looked back over his shoulder at Brad – as if to make sure he was still there. From the doorway where he sat, arms huddled around his knees, Brad said he could see the kids walking into the park across the street with his bike.

"As soon as they were out of sight, Brad ran home. He burst through the front door of their house red-faced and gasping for breath. His mom said he looked like he had been chased by an entire army. His blood-shot eyes were popping out of his head. Immediately, both of his parents asked him what was wrong. Brad just shook his head. His mom wanted to know where the groceries were, and then when he didn't answer, his dad wanted to know if he'd had an accident. But Brad wouldn't tell them anything. He was terrified that Nelson and his gang would find him and carry out their threat.

"It actually took George and his wife a good ten minutes to drag the whole story out of Brad. And when George found out that his son's new bike had been stolen right from under his nose, he was furious. He ran out of the house swearing. Brad followed him crying, begging his dad not to get involved, because he knew Nelson would find him and kill him. This just made George more angry. He said, 'No punk's going to steal my son's bike, threaten him with his life and get away with it! You stay here with your mom – I'm going down to that park to get your bike back. It's time they learned that bullying won't work in this neighbourhood.'

"At the park, George saw the four kids hanging around the water fountain and the red bike lying on the grass a few feet away. Mad as hell, George strode over to the fountain area, ready to teach them a lesson. They were just skinny little kids. The oldest was probably 17. The heaviest was probably about 140 pounds. George himself weighed in at 205 pounds. He'd played football in college and, to tell the truth, had been in more than a few fights in his younger days. He didn't think he'd have a problem getting the bike back.

"He pointed at the biggest kid, who turned out to be Nelson and screamed, 'Hey, you! That bike over there belongs to my son.' The four kids stopped talking and just looked over at him.

"Nelson looked up from his chest and smiled. 'I don't know what you're talking about, man. That bike right there is my friend's brother's. You can't take that.' And as he finished his sentence he stood up as tall as he could. Behind him, the other kids started pacing and acting more agitated. What George didn't know was that they were psyching themselves up. They were bristling, which is the aggressive or nervous behaviour that usually signals a gang or group is about to get violent.

"Outraged that he was hearing this from a skinny, high-school kid, George stepped closer to Nelson, getting right in his face. Nelson didn't flinch. Pointing at the kid's chest, George said, 'My son just came running home in tears. He says you hit him and this is definitely his bike. I'm taking it back and don't you ever, I mean ever, go near my kid again or I swear I'll beat you to within in an inch of your life.'

"Nelson just smiled and stared straight into George's face. Thinking that he'd made his point, George stepped around Nelson and walked over to the bike. Behind him he could hear the other kids clucking and making noises, laughing loud enough for him to hear. He bent over at the waist to pick the bike up off the grass and just as his hand closed around the handlebars, something heavy and solid smacked into the back of his head. George went down like a ton of bricks. He fell onto the bike and cut his shoulder deeply. Blood poured out onto his chest. Looking up, trying hard to focus his eyesight, pain throbbing in his temples and neck, George saw all four kids standing over him. He tried to get to his feet but his knees buckled and with a lurch he sat down hard on the grass. The kids were laughing hysterically as Nelson stepped forward and said, 'Take your bike home and if I see you again, you're dead.' Then he hit George again, this time with his fist – right on the side of the head.

"When George came to, he was lying in a bed in the emergency room of the local hospital. A couple walking their dog in the park had seen what happened and had called 911. After hitting George, Nelson and the others had run like hell and disappeared into a maze of alleys behind the houses across the street. By the time the police arrived they were long gone.

"George did recover. He had a bad concussion, needed stitches and had to stay the night in the hospital, but there was no permanent damage. I think he was lucky.

"Eventually, we did arrest Nelson on another charge and, since he matched George's description, we were able to connect him to the bike theft and the assault as well. Nelson ended up doing six months in jail. But the bottom line in this case is that what George did was very dangerous."

11

What We Can All Do To Reduce The Number Of Offenders

❝ As I mentioned earlier, tonight we're going to be talking about what we can all do to reduce the number of offenders. There are two parts to this. First, we'll be dealing with the question of whether or not you should intervene when you see kids causing trouble. Then later in the meeting, we'll develop a list of things we can all do to reduce the number of offenders.

Should You Intervene When You See Kids Causing Trouble?

"I started off tonight by telling George's story because I think it should be a warning to all parents. For the rest of this evening we're going to be talking about a lot of different ways to intervene and stop youth violence. But never forget that you must always, always make your own personal safety — and the safety of your children – your number one priority. And you should be aware that what I'm going to tell you about intervention and safety is just my opinion. To get a more complete idea of how to protect yourself, you should also talk to street-smart experts and self-defense trainers. I think that discussing the assault on George will give us some basic strategies to ensure that we remain safe and help us break the Violence Ladder.

"So, let's start thinking about George and how he handled the situation with Nelson. Since George ended up in the hospital, I think we need to start our discussion by answering a very big question – should parents get involved in violent situations the way George did? Any opinions?"

Lydia put her hand up and said, "I'm not sure what to think, Kevin. I mean, I think kids like Nelson need to be dealt with, but, frankly, after hearing George's story and all the other stories you've told us this year, I'm terrified. Maybe parents shouldn't get involved in situations like that anymore. We've talked a lot this year about how different the world is today compared to when we were kids. Maybe it's no longer possible for parents to step in and deal with these young offenders."

"I agree, Lydia," I said. "As you said, the first of our three most important points to understand about youth violence is that our children's world is radically different from the one we grew up in. Things have changed on the street. And, as we discussed in September and October, that's true of every neighbourhood in every city across the country. I've been telling you stories for months that illustrate just how drastically things have changed.

"Nowadays, the small percentage of kids who are hard-core offenders behave more violently than they ever did before. They're more likely to lash out at each other and even adults. A significant number of them are even carrying weapons. So, stepping into a situation with young offenders can be dangerous. George's incident is rather extreme, but it illustrates what can happen when parents try to deal with a gang of kids. If the situation is not handled correctly, adults can get sucked into a spiraling series of threats that can erupt into violence and weapons use. We have even had uniformed police officers getting swarmed and assaulted by youth gangs in public.

"Having said that, however, I still strongly believe that parents play the most important role in reducing youth violence. For too long we've left our children unattended, so to speak. And a big reason why things are worse now than they were a generation or two ago is that parents stopped getting involved. If my parents saw a kid littering or bullying, they would put a stop to it. Kids respected adults – even if those adults weren't their own parents. But we as parents don't have that kind of control over our streets anymore – we've given it up to the kids. And it will be hard to win that control back.

"That's why, when we encounter young offenders in a violent situation, we need to be able to tell when it is safe for us to intervene, and we should have a clear idea of what we are attempting to accomplish by doing so.

WHEN IS IT SAFE FOR PARENTS TO INTERVENE IN VIOLENT SITUATIONS?

"In order to figure out whether to jump into a situation like George did, or to take another approach, there are 2 simple questions that you should ask yourself before you do anything. Question 1 – Will you be safe? And, Question 2 – Even if you are safe, will you be breaking the Violence Ladder?

QUESTION 1: WILL YOU BE SAFE?

"Before George confronted Nelson he should have asked himself if he was compromising his personal safety. Obviously, he didn't stop to consider that and the reality was that he was in jeopardy. Consequently, he ended up in the hospital with serious head injuries.

ARE YOU ALONE OR OUTNUMBERED?

"Because George was facing a group of kids by himself, he should have realized immediately that he was in danger. Instead, he relied on his size and a groundless belief that these were just kids — kids who couldn't hurt him. As we discussed earlier, that belief is no longer true. The newspapers are filled with stories about adults who are mugged or beaten or swarmed by gangs of kids. In many cases, a gang of fourteen-year-olds can be more dangerous than several adults.

ARE THE KIDS BRISTLING OR ACTING AGGRESSIVELY?

"Even though George didn't consider his personal safety before he approached Nelson and the other kids, he should have been wary when they started agitating and bouncing around and bristling. As I mentioned in the story, bristling is an aggressive or nervous behaviour that gang members display immediately before a confrontation or an assault. They bounce around in tight circles, strut, flash hand signs to each other. If you ever find yourself faced with a group of kids who suddenly begin bristling, leave right away. Don't make the same mistake as George.

WHO'S TURF ARE YOU ON — YOURS OR THEIRS?

"Another thing that George didn't consider was the setting – and this dramatically affected his safety. Think back to the story. George was the one who went after Nelson and his gang, and found them in a park. In effect, he was confronting them on their own turf, which is never a good idea. A group of kids or even a single hard-core offender will become very territorial if you approach them in a place they consider to be theirs. You are intruding, and they will fight you off. Effectively, you will have very little power there – they simply won't listen to you. Conversely, if kids are causing trouble on your property or on your street, then you have the upper hand. This is your turf, and it's up to you to make sure that it remains a safe haven for your kids.

ARE THESE KIDS STRANGERS TO YOU?

"A terrible mistake that George made was confronting kids he didn't know. If you remember, he rushed over to the park in a blind rage and began aggressively arguing and threatening the kids who'd stolen his son's bike. But he had no idea who they were. He didn't know their parents, where they lived, what kind of kids they were. He had no idea whether or not they had police records or a reputation for violent behaviour. They were total unknowns as far as George was concerned. Never, under any circumstances, intervene in a situation involving strange kids.

"Always take a good look at any kids you approach and try to remember if you've seen them in your neighbourhood before. If you know them or know their parents, then they are more likely to listen to you.

YOU CAN'T TELL IF A KID IS VIOLENT FROM THE WAY THEY ARE DRESSED

"If you don't recognize them, don't make the mistake of thinking you can tell what they're like from their clothes or manner. That's a mistake a lot of people make. The truth is there isn't always a correlation between attitude and dress and behaviour. After all, look at the adult criminals like The Preppy Murderer or Paul Bernardo. Would you have guessed they were serial killers from looking at them or talking to them for 30 seconds? There really is no dress code for criminals.

ARE THERE WEAPONS INVOLVED?

"The final thing I want you to consider is the presence of weapons. In George's case he didn't see whatever they hit him with, so he had no way of knowing the dangers in advance. You can never tell for sure if someone is carrying a concealed weapon. But, in situations where you see that a gun or a knife or any kind of weapon is involved, you must never intervene. Call the police. Do not jeopardize your safety.

IF YOU CANNOT GUARANTEE YOUR OWN SAFETY CALL THE POLICE

"Asking the questions that I've just listed will help you determine if you are safe. If you cannot guarantee your own safety or that of your child, do not get involved. Clearly, George should not have taken matters into his own hands. He should not have tried to deal with Nelson alone. And in a similar situation, you shouldn't either. This doesn't mean walking away and locking yourself and your kids in the house. It means letting the proper people do their job. Call the police, the school, or the kids' parents if you know them. The key is to communicate, because communication and teamwork break the Violence Ladder. As we saw time and time again in Chris's story, Jamie's story, and David's story, the proper authorities need to be made aware of the problem so that they can deal with it effectively. Only then will the Violence Ladder be broken.

"The Violence Ladder is likely to take over if we don't talk to each other and instead try to handle situations on our own. Harassment can become threats, groups can form, weapons might appear and ultimately violence may result. We've spent a long time talking about this with reference to our children, stressing the importance of educating them to come and tell us when they are faced with a situation in which violence may develop. This is no less true for ourselves. Don't try to resolve a criminal situation by yourself. I can't emphasize enough that people are getting killed because they don't stop to think. Be careful. If the situation is too dangerous, call the police.

QUESTION 2: EVEN IF YOU ARE SAFE, WILL YOU BE BREAKING THE VIOLENCE LADDER?

"Even if you are confident that it is safe for you to intervene, I feel it is crucial for you to also consider whether or not your actions will help break the Violence Ladder. In other words, are you finding a solution to the problem, or becoming part of it?

DON'T USE VIOLENCE TO SOLVE PROBLEMS

"As a parent you are a role model, it's vitally important that your children don't see you solving problems through the use of violence. That is one of the big mistakes George made. Brad did his part in trying to break the Violence Ladder – he came home and told his parents about the threats and the theft, but, instead of acting responsibly, George ran off ready to do battle – perpetuating the escalation of violence. Even if he had wrestled the bike from the kids and not been hurt, there would have been ramifications. George could have been charged with assault himself, or the kids could have sought revenge.

"Never participate in any of the steps on the Violence Ladder yourself. Don't harass, or threaten, or use weapons, or act violently. Never try to be a cowboy by taking the law into your own hands. It has taken me nine years of training and daily experience as a police officer to learn to deal with these types of situations, and they are still dangerous.

DON'T REACT EMOTIONALLY

"Your aim should always be to break the Violence Ladder, and the key to making that happen is to stop and think. Don't just react the way George did. Try not to be emotional. Don't let anger colour your decisions. Objectively consider whether what you want to do is going to stop the escalation of violence or contribute to it."

I paused for a second and looked around the room. "The two things I want to stress with regard to reacting to young offenders are: only intervene if you are safe, and only if your actions will break the Violence Ladder. Does anybody have any stories of their own they'd like to share?"

SAUL GETS SWARMED

Lydia spoke up from her seat near the back, "I'd just like to echo what Kevin was saying. The story that he told about George doesn't seem so farfetched to me, because I've heard of similar things happening to friends of mine. A guy that my husband and I know, Saul, was involved in an incident with a group of kids last summer while he was playing tennis and it scared the crap out of him. Saul is a very fit, massive 42-year-old and he was just dealing with a group of fourteen-year-old kids – but they really put a scare into him."

"What happened?" I asked.

"It was in the summer and he'd called up a friend of his, Earl, to play tennis," Lydia said. "It was probably about five or six o'clock at night, and still very light out because it was July. Anyway, when Saul and Earl got to the two courts there were two women playing on one court and on the other court there were about fifteen kids – all of them running around with rackets, smashing balls over the fence, screaming and swearing and chasing each other. Now, the rule is that after a half hour on the court you have to come off and let the next group come on. So Saul and Earl put their rackets on the board and sat down to wait. And the whole time they were waiting, these kids were goofing around. They were even running all over the other court where the two women were trying to play a game. Saul said he could see the two women getting increasingly angry, but obviously too afraid to say anything.

"When the half hour was up, Saul and Earl stood up and went over to the kids' court ready to play, but the kids didn't stop horsing around. So Saul said, 'Excuse me, you guys have to give up the courts now.' and pointed to the sign. The kids on the court didn't even look up, they just laughed.

"At that point, two of the kids chased each other into the other court, ruining the rally the women were having. Without thinking, Saul ran over to the two kids and let them have it. He told them to grow up and have some consideration for the other people on the courts, the ones who were actually trying to play a game. And then he said, 'If you want to just run around like idiots why don't you go and do it on the grass.' There was lots of room in the nearby park for kids to play.

"Suddenly all the kids froze. But instead of being scared, they all started walking over towards Saul and Earl. At the time, Saul thought, well, they're only about 14-years-old. But he did start to get nervous as they closed around him in a circle. Then the biggest of the kids, who was only as tall as Saul's shoulder, came over, told Saul to screw off, and started jabbing him in the chest. Saul told the kid to back off, but that only made him more agitated. All of the other kids began to crowd in around them, banging their rackets on the concrete and yelling at the top of their lungs. From behind Saul, Earl shouted for the two of them to get out of there, then pushed through the kids and dragged Saul out onto the street. Fortunately, Saul and Earl left and that was the end of it."

"That story, Lydia," I said, "is a great example of why you should always be extremely careful in those situations. Although those kids were probably less than half Saul's size, they clearly outnumbered Saul and Earl, and could have easily hurt them both. The bottom-line for me is — I'm a cop and I would never have done what Saul did. Following that incident they definitely should have called the police."

Robert put up his hand and said, "Kevin, you've been stressing how dangerous it can be to get involved but, come on, they're just kids. I think we need to teach them a lesson, show them that we're not afraid to discipline them. As you said, we need to establish control of our streets and neighbourhoods. Unless the kid has a gun or maybe a knife, I don't think I'd hesitate to get involved. . . ."

WENDY TAKES BACK HER STREET

Before I could respond, Wendy jumped in with an answer, "Well, I've never, you know, wrestled a robber to the ground or snatched a gun off some masked hoodlum, Robert, but sometimes there are kids on our street who are just having a thrill – you know getting into mischief. I've dealt with them before."

"And what happened?" I asked.

"One afternoon in the summer, I was out watering the lawn. Some of my neighbours were also out on their porches or lawns. There must have been at least a half dozen people outside. Anyway, it was a Monday – garbage day and the truck had already been around to pick up everyone's trash, but a lot of the empty garbage cans were still out by the road.

"All of a sudden there was a colossal banging and clattering noise, like metal being hammered. Everyone who was outside looked up. About a block down the street there was a group of kids – three kids actually –wrestling and rolling around on the grass between the sidewalk and the road. They had rolled into the garbage cans in front of that house and knocked them into the road – where they were still rolling around.

"They were just play fighting I think, because they broke apart a couple of seconds later and, leaving the metal trash cans in the middle of the street, they started running down the sidewalk in my direction. And every time they passed empty garbage bins, they'd speed up and race each other to kick them out into the street."

"So, what were your neighbours doing?" I asked. "This was right on your own street, your turf, so to speak. And there were quite a few adults around. Did someone stop them?"

"Well, that's the crazy thing. My neighbours all just stood around and watched," she said, her voice rising a little in pitch and her eyebrows lifting in surprise. "They were making a shambles of our street and no one said a thing. By the time they got to my house, I'd had enough. When they got closer, I realized they weren't all complete strangers to me. A couple of the faces looked familiar. I think they live on the next block. I've seen one of them walking with his parents a couple of times. Anyway, I've never tried to discipline anyone else's kids before, but I couldn't let those little brats get away with what they were doing. It was irresponsible and dangerous. I was so mad that I didn't even think about the consequences of getting involved – I just threw down my garden hose and screamed, 'Hey, what do you think you're doing?!? What if a car hits one of those garbage cans? What if someone gets hurt?' It wasn't until the first few words were out of my mouth that I began to realize what I was doing. Even as I was talking I could feel myself growing more nervous. Suddenly my initial anger ebbed and I started to get scared. Even though they were only 14 or so, I thought, 'Oh no – what if they turn on me?' I was worried they were going to hurt me or do something to my house."

"And what did they do?" I asked. I knew from experience that these types of situations could very easily explode. These days kids do fight back. In many cases they certainly don't have the respect for adults, or property or safety that we had as children.

"I picked up a rake that had been lying in the grass beside me," Wendy said. "My knuckles were white. Suddenly I was scared to death. My breath was coming in heaves and my legs felt like Jell-O. But what really shocked me was that the three of them just stopped dead. They froze! Right there on the sidewalk. And, you know, when I looked at them, standing on the sidewalk in front of my house, in the middle of the block-long mess of garbage cans, I saw them as they actually were – not tough, young offenders or violent outlaws. They were kids, fourteen-year-old kids who were bored and unsupervised."

"What did they do after you yelled at them, Wendy?" I asked.

"Oh, they apologized. One of them, the smallest one, looked like he was going to cry. It was so sad. His eyes were huge and watery and his face was all red. The older one, he was wearing a big T-shirt and these baggy jeans – he was just lost inside his clothes – anyway, he stammered that they were sorry. They were just goofing around, he said. And it sounded so pathetic. In just two minutes my emotions had gone from anger to fear to sympathy. I actually felt sorry for them and it was hard, you know, to keep up a stern face. But, I was supposed to be teaching them a lesson – so I had them walk back down the street and pick up the garbage cans, and I watched them the entire time."

"You were lucky that they were just harmless kids play-fighting," I said, "and not kids with a more dangerous intent. But I do commend you on taking action. You were on your own street, in public, with lots of help nearby so it wasn't such a bad decision. It shows that you are proud of your neighbourhood and want to preserve its security. In fact, it's a good example of community ownership which is a concept that I try to stress whenever I speak to parents or kids. There were, in fact, more parents around then kids. And you did recognize a couple of them. That's no guarantee, of course, but, I think it does help. In my experience, kids seem to get into more trouble when they are away from home. The key point is that being from the neighbourhood, these kids were probably aware that you knew their parents and that you would report them. It's good to see that somebody is standing up for their neighbourhood. I do caution you, though, to make certain you don't react emotionally in the future. I know it's hard, but try to remain cool. You'll be safer that way."

Turning to face Robert, I said, "So there's an example of an intervention that worked, Robert. There were no weapons involved, it occurred on Wendy's street and no crime was actually being committed."

Turning back to Wendy, I said, "I bet the other people on the street were pleased about that, Wendy."

"Yeah," she agreed, "and what surprised me even more was that, since I pulled that little stunt, I've noticed that the other parents on the street are much more aggressive and active in policing the neighbourhood. It's like they're not as afraid any more. I think they realize that something has to be done and, most importantly, that we're all in this together. Just like kids get their confidence to cause trouble because they are part of a group, the parents on my street now have the confidence to confront troublemakers because they feel they'll get some support if they need it."

I nodded, "Yes, that's an interesting thing that happens when adults in a community begin to intervene and deal with problem situations. Establishing or reinforcing norms for our neighbourhoods and communities is really what we're doing when we intervene in situations, even incidents as petty as the one you had with those kids who were knocking over the garbage cans.

"And by it's very nature, reinforcing those norms is a group effort," I continued. "We can all act individually as parents or members of the community, but it is important to know that we have the support of our neighbours and friends.

PARENTS RALLY BEHIND CLIFF

"For instance, near my home there's a guy with a corner house, right by the stop sign. He has kids and so do a few other families on his block, and it makes him crazy when drivers go speeding down his street, or even worse, don't stop at the stop sign. And he's right, the kids play outside and it's dangerous. The thing is, this guy sits on his porch in the summer and whenever he sees a car flying down the road or rolling through the intersection, he jumps out of his seat and starts yelling at them. One time, a big kid in a Mustang, maybe sixteen, came rocketing down the street and, as he flew by, Cliff jumped up and started screaming and waving his hands at the guy. This time though, the kid must have thought he was a tough guy, and he slammed on the brakes, bringing the car to a screeching halt. The door flew open and he unfolded his massive frame from the driver's seat, already yelling at Cliff. Cliff yelled back and the kid started walking menacingly towards Cliff's porch. But then, all of a sudden, from half the houses on the block, men and women came down from their porches one by one and started walking over to Cliff's lawn. Of course, seeing that he wasn't dealing with just a 50-year-old man anymore, the kid turned and ran back to his car and no one's seen that Mustang since.

"Although Cliff was concerned for his safety, he was reacting emotionally, and as we have said, when confronting strangers there is always the possibility of violence. But, what's interesting to me about that story is the way that a group of parents showing support for each other were able to break the Violence Ladder."

I paused for a second before moving on. "Okay," I said, "I want to summarize on the blackboard the points about when you should and shouldn't confront a young offender.

THE SAFETY CHECKLIST

"So – when you encounter a situation involving young offenders, what's the first question you should always ask yourself?" I asked.

"Is it safe to intervene?" Mary called out.

"Good," I said, writing the question on the blackboard, "and how will you know if it is safe?"

"You need to go through the checklist," Lydia said. "Are you alone? Are you outnumbered? Do you recognize any of the kids? Is a crime taking place? Is violence involved? Are weapons involved? Are you on their turf?"

"Right. Anything else?" I asked, writing the key words on the blackboard as she spoke.

"What about bristling," said Ian, "and make sure that you recognize them from the neighbourhood."

"There," I said, adding the last two items to the list under the heading of safety. "That's all the points we got from George's story about safety. What's the other major question to ask yourself before you intervene?" I asked.

"If you are successful, will you be breaking the Violence Ladder?" said Wendy.

I wrote that on the board and underlined it and turned back to face the room. "Those are the major things to remember when reacting to kids who are committing a crime or being anti-social. But as I said, the key to dealing with offenders is prevention.

10 THINGS WE CAN ALL DO TO REDUCE THE NUMBER OF OFFENDERS

"Last month we developed a list of things we can all do at home to protect our kids. Tonight, though, I want us to develop a list of things we should all be doing to reduce the number of offenders. And by 'all' I mean all parents, not just the parents in this room. In other words, think beyond your own home. Let's try and develop solutions that should be followed in every home in the country. This way, once you know the solutions, you as parents and as citizens of your community can make the effort to see that our children are raised properly. I should point out that some of the ideas we developed last month will apply here as well. I think we should include them in tonight's list, but develop them further in the context of preventing offending behaviour.

"Perhaps we can start by drawing on some of the stories we've discussed over the year. Can anyone help us out here?"

SOLUTION 1: TEACH CHILDREN TO BE INDIVIDUALS AND MAKE SMART CHOICES

Robert spoke up from the back of the room, "How about that story about the kid, I think his name was Chris, who stabbed the other kid in the subway – we decided that it's important to teach our kids to be individuals and to always remember that they can choose not to become involved in a gang or violent activity."

"That's right, it was also Solution 8 of 'Things you can do at home to protect your kids' and as I said last month it is well worth repeating." I turned and wrote today's first solution on the blackboard – 'Teach children to be individuals and make smart choices.' "And if you remember," I continued, "Chris got caught up in the excitement and commotion in the subway car and stabbed a kid. That's an example of a good kid, someone who was not at all a hard-core young offender, being manipulated by a gang. They preyed on his weakness – his inability to evaluate what he was being told in a mature fashion. He was scared and reacted badly. Instead of reporting the initial threats that he received, he did what the gang told him to do and, in effect, he became their unwitting weapon. He responded to the comfort and sense of belonging that he felt when Stick, the gang leader, approached him. He became a victim because Stick was smart enough to know how a kid like Chris would respond to peer pressure. If Chris had acted as an individual and spoken to his parents or the school staff, the Violence Ladder could have been broken and the stabbing may never have occurred. Certainly, Chris wouldn't have been arrested.

"Think back to when you were young. I'm sure most of us felt a pretty powerful need to belong. And lots of us are probably ashamed to admit we were once victims of many trends – perms, bell-bottoms, disco. It may be harmless to dress like your friends and listen to the same music, but when a child loses the ability to think for himself and blindly goes along with everything that another kid tells him, then the potential for violence rises. They lose the ability to properly evaluate situations and they make stupid choices.

"Recently, another local high-school kid was stabbed in a subway fight and this time he was killed. The students at that school were shocked by what had happened and it really forced them to take stock of how they were acting and how that may have contributed to their friend's death. In fact, I was at that very school presenting my *Tackle Violence* program to the kids just before the stabbing. When I made the point that kids need to make smart choices and walk away from confrontations instead of continuing the escalation of violence, several students at the back of the auditorium laughed and snorted. Now, the concerned students have made a point of speaking up whenever they feel that other students are doing something unacceptable. It's unfortunate that it took a death to encourage kids to speak out against their friends and risk being alienated from their peer group. And it's good to know that when concerned kids speak out others do listen. If all parents could instill the courage to speak out in their kids then we would go a long way toward reducing violence – and kids like Chris would make the right choice instead of ending up in jail.

SOLUTION 2: TEACH KIDS THE CONSEQUENCES OF VIOLENCE

INDESTRUCTIBLE KIDS

"Perhaps the most frightening consequence of kids not thinking for themselves is the attitude that violence is acceptable and cool. And that's why we try to break the Violence Ladder by making violent responses to any situation unacceptable.

"I think at this point we should take some time to look at why kids have this idea that violence is a solution to their problems. I've spoken to a lot of kids who have really unusual and destructive ideas about what it takes to survive in the world today – kids who think that graffiti is artwork not vandalism, that gangs are cool, that shooting or stabbing another kid is brave. The hard-core offenders that I meet say they're not afraid of anything. Even though they face gang fights, knives and guns, they say that fear is for losers and they truly believe that only the coldest and the toughest will survive. In fact, they feel that fear equals respect. Last week, a high-school student told me, 'If I beat him down, he respects me.' I'm talking about kids who are 16 or 13 or even 8 years old.

"A while ago I was at a high school in the north end of the city speaking to a group of about fifteen students as part of their human relations course. Most of the kids were known to the teachers as troublemakers. I asked them if they knew students who carried weapons. They just shrugged and said, 'Yeah, sure.' I asked them if they had ever brought weapons to school and a few of them had. I asked them if they were worried that they could get hurt or even killed, and they all just laughed. They truly believe that they are indestructible. Their heroes are the gang members they see on TV who walk through a hail of bullets without getting hurt, who control their turf through intimidation and violence. They wouldn't admit that there was anything wrong with their way of thinking.

"As a group they were cool and strong. But, interestingly, when the hour was up and they all left, one of them, a big guy who had just grunted and slouched through the whole class, left his friends in the hall and came back into the classroom alone. He looked kind of embarrassed and kept checking to see that his friends weren't watching. Finally, he stuck out his hand and mumbled, 'Hey, thanks for coming, officer – see you later.'

MEDIA: WHERE THE KIDS GET THEIR MESSAGES

"There is a giant barrier between the way we parents think of violence and the way kids like those in the human relations class do. This is the barrier we have to break through. But in order to do so we first need to understand where these kids are coming from." I looked around at the parents and asked, "Where did they get the idea that violence is a solution to their problems?"

Ian raised his hand in the back. "TV," he said. "TV is to blame for this. Kids think they're living in some *Die Hard* movie or a cartoon or something. These kids don't think violence has any consequences. They think that people don't get hurt when they get shot. They really believe what they see and it gives them an attitude. It's scary. How do we fight TV?"

"You know," I said, "you're right about the violence on TV. Personally, I find it too frustrating even to watch the news on most nights. It can sometimes look like everything has slipped out of control. TV violence even extends into kids cartoons and music videos. But it's not just TV. A lot of our culture is fixated on violence – lots of books, movies, and music send the message that it's cool to be tough and that violence is a solution to one's problems. A lot of kids are listening to music that says it's okay or even desirable to take a life or to live like a gangster.

"I just read an article called 'The Impact of Televised Violence,' by Dr. John Murray, a professor and the director of the School of Family Studies and Human Services at Kansas State University. In the article he discusses a recent study that says kids in North America are watching an average of 25 hours of television a week and that a child will see on average 10,000 murders, rapes and assaults every year on TV. A small child sees 25 violent acts every hour in Saturday-morning cartoons, and by the time that child becomes a teenager they will have seen more than 100,000 violent acts. Unfortunately, like every generation of kids in the past forty years, our children have grown up in a world that is defined by the images they see on TV and the lyrics they hear in music. So how does that prepare someone for the stresses of high school? Obviously the various media are showing these kids that if you have a conflict with someone, you get physical. And young kids are naive – they believe what they see and hear. They just don't have the maturity to determine what is right or wrong, real or unreal. Psychologically they aren't completely able to distinguish between the cartoon world of the Mighty Morphin' Power Rangers and the hard, concrete world of the school yard."

As I paused to sip from my coffee, I let my eyes wander around the room. It was quiet. In the front row, Wendy looked down at the desktop in front of her. Beside her Lydia said, "So, what can we do exactly?"

"Well, personally, I think that if we all grew up on the same steady diet of violence and abuse that today's kids do, we'd be having trouble too.

And I don't think that TV or music or whatever are going to get any more responsible any time soon. So we need to get at the source of the problem, which means parents need to teach their kids about the consequences of violence."

On the blackboard I wrote, 'Teach kids the consequences of violence,' and then continued, "What I mean is that parents have to make a point of teaching their children at a very early age that people can be hurt or killed. Kids need to understand that pain and suffering – not glory and success – result from violent behaviour. The key to the entire problem is that adults need to understand that children are immature and largely unable to make good decisions when conflicts arise. So we need to make sure they are prepared. Parents must coach them and make sure that their default behaviour – the one they fall back on when trouble erupts – is a positive one. Instead of lashing out or grouping together with friends to fight an enemy, or getting and using a weapon, kids must understand that the only acceptable solution is to break the Violence Ladder. To do this, they need to resolve conflicts peacefully, or, if they can't, they need to report what happened to somebody who can."

SOLUTION 3: PLAN AND MONITOR TV WATCHING

Ian spoke up again, "That's great, Kevin, but can't we also limit the amount of time our kids spend watching TV and listening to music. My wife and I keep an eye on our kids' TV habits. Plus, we try to make sure that they're watching something appropriate to their age. If we all did that, I think the attitude toward violence might change for the better."

"Well," I replied, "that's another good point. We must reduce the amount of time our kids spend in front of the TV and monitor what they actually watch." Turning to the blackboard I wrote, 'Plan and monitor TV watching.'

"You have to be aware of every show they watch, what it's about, and how you feel about it. If you think that a particular show is unsuitable for your kids, don't let them watch it. There is a concept called Planned TV Watching that I think is very effective in helping families manage their child's viewing time. Basically it involves following a few simple rules. If you don't want your kid watching TV, don't laze around in front of it yourself. Plan other activities for the whole family at times when your children would otherwise be watching the tube. Don't put a TV in your child's bedroom. Plan your TV watching for the day or even the week. When the particular show that you wanted to watch is over, then turn off the TV. It also helps to have rules about not watching the television at meal times or even on school nights."

SOLUTION 4: SET FIRM BOUNDARIES FOR CHILDREN AND ENFORCE THEM

Before I'd finished, Mary said, "Oh, come on, Kevin, they won't go for that. You know how kids – especially teenagers – are always pushing back. They don't stand still for rules and boundaries like that."

"Well, you're certainly right about that," I said, "but I think that just because they rebel against your authority – as kids tend to do – that doesn't mean you should give up and stop providing them with guidance. On the contrary, it's at exactly that time that they need your help the most. We need to establish limits to our children's behaviour." I wrote, 'Set firm boundaries for children and enforce them,' on the blackboard.

"In the *Youth Gangs on Youth Gangs* book by Fred Mathews, the kids themselves say that the number-one thing that they need from their parents is structure and discipline. Even though kids know that they will test the limits you set, they still believe they need them. For their sake, we have to be strong and persevere – it's our responsibility as parents.

"Without strict limits, kids can go astray. Whenever they get away with something, they'll try and take it a step further the next time. If they come home late by fifteen minutes one night without a word from their parents, then next week they'll try half an hour. If we don't set and enforce boundaries then very quickly we lose control. And we can't hand over control to our kids completely because they just aren't mature enough to be responsible for everything in their lives.

"One way that kids test the limits is to try to divert blame away from themselves if they are caught or accused of something. Often they will say 'My friend made me do it' or claim that 'The principal is a liar.' Really they're pushing to see if you will take the easy way out. And parents must be careful to hold them accountable to the rules they have established. If their kid gives them a reason or an excuse for stepping over the boundaries, then the parents should make sure they are critical of what their kid is saying. Their story may be the truth, but it may just as easily be a diversion. Many parents are too willing to believe everything their kids say.

And as a result, rules and boundaries become meaningless because consequences are never enforced when they need to be."

At that point Mary put up her hand and said, "In one of the earlier meetings you said that parents should be supportive of their kids and to listen to what they tell them. Now I'm hearing that parents should be more like enforcers. What's right? What should parents do if, for instance, one of their children gets into serious trouble? Say they were charged with assault – what should parents do then?"

"As I just said, I think there is a large problem with parents who deny that their kid could have done anything wrong. They choose to believe only the best about their child, even if they are brought home by the police, or arrested, or suspended. A lot of parents just want the problem to go away – they want to pay the fine and sweep the whole issue under the carpet. This is the wrong attitude. On the other hand, parents shouldn't go off half-cocked and scream or abuse their kid.

"The key to solving this problem is establishing boundaries or rules that are fair to everyone. But then parents have to be firm in enforcing those rules. So, when a child is arrested, parents should make sure their kid understands that what they did was wrong. They should make it clear that they are not impressed and should make sure that the kid completes the sentence passed by the court, whether that is community service or whatever.

"On the flip side of that, how would you feel if your kid became the victim of school-yard harassment or violence and the offender was not punished? As you can imagine, if the victims don't see any recourse or action taken when they report what happened to them, they will either give up completely and become repeat victims or they will go elsewhere looking for a response.

THE YOUNG OFFENDER'S ACT IS NOT A DETERRENT

"For a long time, we have relied on the courts, the police and the law to establish boundaries strong enough to keep our children from committing crimes. We have assumed that the penalty for breaking the law is frightening or severe enough that it will actually prevent people from breaking the law. The problem is kids no longer see the Criminal Code as a deterrent. Today, they think they can hide behind the law because they're under the impression that the Young Offender's Act protects them from prosecution.

"It's true that children under age 12 can't be charged for a criminal act. In many cases it's difficult to prosecute kids who are 16 and 17 as adults and impose stiff penalties, no matter what the offense. These kids aren't stupid. They're aware of exactly how far they can push authority and the law. They know that they can't be charged as criminals until they reach age 12. And, as a result, young, hard-core offenders behave as if they're untouchable. Basically, they think the Young Offender's Act is a joke.

"The papers and the nightly news shows are full of examples of this attitude. Recently, an 11-year-old boy who allegedly raped a 13-year-old girl couldn't be charged with an offense because he was too young. And another 11-year-old was caught holding up a downtown store with a sawed-off shotgun and couldn't be charged. A ten-year-old, repeatedly arrested for breaking into homes and cars, once told the arresting officers, 'Yeah, you caught me. But you can't do nothing about it.' The fact that there are absolutely no criminal consequences for their behaviour makes these kids think that anything is possible –this is completely unacceptable.

"As for kids who are subject to the YOA, I personally see the problem as being one of education. In my opinion, kids perceive that the Young Offender's Act is weak and ineffectual. They think it has no teeth and doesn't allow the courts to punish children who commit crime. This is not actually true, but if that's what the kids believe, then we have a problem. It doesn't matter what the reality is – if they think they won't suffer any consequences, they will continue to commit crimes. They are, in fact, using the Young Offender's Act as an excuse for violent or criminal behaviour.

"In the *Youth Gangs on Youth Gangs* study that I talked about earlier, the adults who where interviewed did agree that the Act should be reviewed and strengthened if necessary. However, the biggest need is to make kids aware that they can and will be prosecuted for criminal offenses. Only if kids believe that, does the Young Offender's Act become an effective deterrent. I've had experience with kids who've told me that a stiffer penalty for their first offense probably would have scared them straight and kept them from continuing to commit crime. So, I think we should increase awareness about the sentences kids receive and promote the successes of the system. This will help deter would-be offenders. And we should also be making sure that the courts impose the penalties that the law allows, instead of letting kids off with warnings and no real punishment. That is a key to reducing the number of offenders. We must remove the perception that in most cases, especially first offenses, the kid will not be sent to jail or punished in any meaningful way.

"The kids themselves – especially the ones who have been through the system and have actually done time for robbery, or murder or some other criminal offense – are quick to point out that very few children have any real knowledge of the legislation. In the *Youth Gangs on Youth Gangs* study, many of the older kids who were interviewed, the ones who were 16, 17, or 18, said that the young, hard-core offender often sees a light sentence as an acceptable trade-off for being able to kill somebody or steal a large amount of money. Even they felt that the Act is too lenient on first time offenders and that it needs to be upgraded in order to serve as an effective deterrent.

"Clearly we have a long way to go before we have an effective way of dealing with young offenders, let alone reducing the number of them. But, if parents, schools, police departments and legislators work together, it is possible to make improvements. For example, the schools that have experimented with 'get-tough' approaches to crime, such as the zero-tolerance programs, have seen their crime rates drop. But I don't want to get into a lot of detail about that now because it is actually the subject of our next meeting.

SOLUTION 5: BE A GOOD ROLE MODEL FOR YOUR KIDS

"We should keep moving and try to capture some more strategies for preventing kids from becoming young offenders. A few moments ago, while we were talking about the problem with television watching, we mentioned how parents should not laze around in front of the TV if they don't want their kids to do so. I think this is actually a very crucial point. Psychologists have shown that children learn a tremendous amount by passively watching other kids or their parents, or, for that matter, TV as well. Therefore, in order to be a good influence on our kids, we must act as role models. If parents want their kids to be confident, independent, thoughtful and careful, then they must show them how. Parents have to display those traits whenever they are with their kids. And, in addition, they must make sure that what they are telling them matches what they do. The cliché here would be 'practice what you preach.' There is nothing more confusing for a kid than hearing that they should never use violence when their father or mother uses threats or even violence to solve problems. If children see their parents behaving this way, they will assume that it is acceptable for them to do the same. We don't want kids to get the idea that violence solves problems – because it doesn't.

I wrote, 'Be a good role model for your kids' on the blackboard.

SOLUTION 6: TEACH KIDS GOOD VALUES AT AN EARLY AGE

To my left, I saw Mary's hand go up. "I think we should take what you're saying a bit further," she said. "It's more than just being a good role model that matters. Parents should be teaching their kids good values – and they should start doing that the day they are born."

"I agree, Mary," I said, turning back to the blackboard and adding, 'Teach kids good values at an early age' to the list. "I think it's absolutely crucial that all parents teach their children sound, pro-social and anti-criminal values before they begin school. A child who has a solid foundation of those kinds of values is much less likely to be lured by others into criminal situations and become an offender. This is common sense stuff, but I think these kinds of values are missing in many kids these days. All parents need to make sure that their children are aware of what is right and wrong and that they are strong enough to make smart choices on their own.

"As a 1995 article in *Psychology Today* called 'Kindergarten Killers' reported, social skills training for children must come early. It does no good to try and teach a young offender acceptable social skills after they have committed a crime. The article said that programs which attempted to retrain convicted young offenders had little success.

"As well, in the *Youth Gangs on Youth Gangs* study, Dr. Mathews reported that, even if kids do get into trouble, a firm base of pro-social values makes it easier for them to find their way back to normal life. In some cases, some members of very hard-core gangs grow up and eventually try to leave, resisting the peer pressure that holds them in the gang. As they mature, they realize the danger they are in, and that gives them the strength to overcome the peer pressure that previously kept them in the gang. However, once they are out on their own, without a support group of friends and a foundation of good values, these kids or young adults can easily turn back into offenders."

SOLUTION 7: BUILD HIGH SELF-ESTEEM

"What about self-esteem, Kevin?" asked Lydia. "We saw in Chris's story that he should have acted as an individual and been strong enough to say no to Stick. But I think he would only have been able to do that if he had healthy self-esteem. Shouldn't parents be making sure their kids are confident and comfortable with themselves from a very early age in order to prevent them from being so easily swayed by offenders?"

I turned and wrote, 'Build high self-esteem.'

"I don't think we can underestimate how important self-esteem is, Lydia," I said. "We saw last month how self-esteem is one of the warning signs of being a victim. And we suggested that building self-esteem was one way of protecting your kid from violence. But, as Lydia suggested, self-esteem is also a key to preventing violent behaviour in kids. There is a group in the States called Mothers Against Gangs that pointed to low self-esteem and a poor outlook on life as key factors that contribute to the high rates of crime and violence committed by young offenders. It really is a crucial point. Parents need to constantly reinforce and support their children. They should ensure that their kids are committed to their education, and they should impress upon them that there is more to life than unemployment or a dead-end job. Kids need to be shown that hard work can be rewarding and that harassment, drug abuse, violence or theft are not legitimate alternatives. Kids should feel good about themselves, they should believe they are capable of reaching goals, and they should know that their parents are there to help them along.

"Personally, I think parents should try almost anything to build their kid's self-esteem. For instance, parents should be getting them involved in sports or clubs and other after-school activities. By developing their interests, kids become more confident in themselves as individuals. They start to see that they can contribute to the world in positive ways. They form friendships with other children who are not at risk of becoming hard-core offenders. And playing sports, in particular, is a great way to channel aggression into healthy competition.

"A recent article in the *Globe and Mail*, for instance, reported that studies have shown that boys with part-time jobs or steady girlfriends are much less likely to become offenders. The responsibility of a job or a relationship means kids have a focus for their energy, and it means that some of their personal needs are being met. A job is especially valuable because it demonstrates to the child that hard work brings money and social standing and other benefits. A kid with a part-time job would be far less likely to need to join a gang for money or respect."

SOLUTION 8: CHALLENGE YOUR KIDS AND LEARN ABOUT THEIR LIFE

Robert's hand suddenly shot up, "I think some of these ideas will be really helpful. But some kids don't seem to want their parents to get involved in their lives. You know, they retreat into their own private worlds. I have a friend, David, for instance. He was telling me that he and his wife are having a really hard time with their 14-year-old boy, Owen. His behaviour is fairly typical of a surly teenager – he doesn't talk to them, he just mumbles all the time. He won't tell them anything about what's happening in his life. Another student and Owen had had a fairly heated rivalry for a couple months, in which they'd got into a few fist-fights. But my friend only learned about it because he happened to overhear Owen discussing it on the phone – and that was weeks after it had all died down."

Wendy spoke up. She said, "Well, I don't think your friend is alone in having that problem, Robert. I think parents really have to be strong with them. It's the same as what Kevin was saying about laying down rules and having them fight back. I'm sure that with a lot of kids when you ask them how their day was, or how they're doing in school, or how they feel, they just grunt or mumble. I know my own son does that sometimes. I guess it's easier not to answer. Many of them are reluctant to let you into their world. And that seems normal to me. After all, they're trying to carve out their own space and make their own way in the world. They're learning to become adults. But that doesn't mean you should leave them alone. So, I would say, tell your friend David to not give up. He should really make a concerted effort to talk with his kids. He should challenge them. He shouldn't accept a mumble or a half-hearted reply. I really think that if you show interest and genuine concern and you are consistent about it, day after day, then it's possible to be close to them."

"A former partner of mine," I said, "has the philosophy that he can't possibly talk to his kids enough. So he's constantly asking them what's going on in their life. He does this because he loves them but also because he strongly believes that it's the easiest way to ensure their safety. And he makes sure that they always feel comfortable talking to him. He's a good example of an educated parent. The fact of the matter is, if you don't know what's happening in your kid's life – with their friends and school – then you're both in danger." I turned to look at Robert. "In the case of your friend David, his son Owen was in jeopardy the whole time he was having that ongoing scrap. I think David's lucky nothing serious happened to Owen."

From the blackboard I said, "I like the way Wendy put it when she said 'challenge' because it gets across the idea that parents have to work hard at having a relationship with their kids. So I'm going to capture the last few things we said as 'Challenge your kids and learn about their life.'

SOLUTION 9: GIVE YOUR KIDS THE ATTENTION THEY NEED

"You know," I said, "I want to add the point that even though kids sometimes shrug their parents off, they still need the attention. In fact, sometimes I think they shrug us off as a test. They want to see if we really care or not. I've spoken to a lot of kids who were once young offenders, and a great many of them feel that the trouble they caused or the crimes they committed were just an attempt to make their families pay attention to them. That certainly doesn't excuse them from their behaviour, but it does point to a solution – parents must give their kids the attention they need. I don't know how many kids have told me that their parents are always working, or preoccupied with the other kids in the family. As a result, a child can grow frustrated and begin to feel that they need to do something dramatic to refocus everyone's attention. That's a dangerous situation with a high potential for violence. And if you remember, in our December meeting we discussed why kids join gangs and saw that gangs can become a substitute family because lots of kids get more attention in a gang than at home.

"When we talked about building self-esteem, we discussed that parents should be encouraging their kids to get involved in sports and activities. But it's just as important that parents get involved in their kids' lives. This came up last month as well, when discussing how to protect your kid from becoming a victim. In fact, we made it one of our solutions and said that parents should get involved with their kids. This is just as true for preventing offenders as it is for preventing victims. All parents should make an effort to coach their son's baseball team or their daughter's soccer team, or drive them out to hockey or dance class once a week. All of this gives kids the attention they need."

I turned to the blackboard and wrote, 'Give your kids the attention they need.'

SOLUTION 10: LEARN ALL YOU CAN ABOUT THE WORLD OUR CHILDREN LIVE IN

"There's another important point to be made here," I said. "Not only do we need to learn about what our children are doing at school, who their friends are and what they do at night when they go out, but we need to be educated about the bigger issue of youth violence in general. As we mentioned in our last meeting, the key to understanding our children's world is getting all the information we can from the schools, police and other organizations in our communities.

"A recent study called *The Badge and the Book*, commissioned by the Ministry of the Solicitor General of Canada, looked at students in schools all across the country and found some remarkably consistent attitudes among our children. A key concern voiced by the kids was that, as a group, parents and educators did not take things like bullying or harassment in the school system seriously enough. They called our attitudes towards the problem of violence in the hallways 'outdated,' and genuinely felt that we had little or no idea about what really went on in their classrooms, school yards and streets on a day-to-day basis.

"The issue of our ignorance of their world came up last month in our discussion on preventing victims. It was important back then because showing our kids we understand their world ensures that they will feel comfortable coming to us for help. They know we will take them seriously. But it's important in the context of preventing offenders as well. If kids think we are out of it, they're more likely to take matters into their own hands. In other words, a lot of them will try and solve their problems the only way they know how – with violence.

"I think it's a great sign that we're all here because that's what this course is all about – learning the 3 most important points about youth violence and breaking the Violence Ladder. That's the education that our children are telling us we need. As the *Youth Gangs on Youth Gangs* study showed, kids feel strongly that adults need to be educated about the presence and danger of youth gangs and the Violence Ladder. I would definitely recommend that everyone here absorb all that they can about the subject of youth violence even after these meetings are over. Read all the books and magazine or newspaper articles you can. The government makes several studies available to the public, you just have to mail away for them. Also, get involved in all the community solutions you can by attending all of the meetings, forums and seminars that are available. It's all about continuing to learn and staying abreast of the current realities and trends in youth crime. I don't think that anybody, the government included, is doing a great job of making sure that parents understand youth violence and are equipped to deal with it, so you really have to be proactive."

I turned and wrote up our last point, 'Learn all you can about the world our children live in.'

SUMMARY

Looking at the blackboard I saw that we had built up quite a long list of ways in which parents could prevent children from becoming offenders. "Well, congratulations," I said. "To me, this is a very solid list. If every parent in the country was able to do all of these things all of the time, I think we wouldn't have much of a problem with young offenders."

THE SAFETY CHECKLIST

QUESTION 1: WILL YOU BE SAFE?

Don't intervene if:

1. You are alone or outnumbered
2. The kids are bristling or acting aggressively
3. You are on their turf or not in a public place
4. The kids are strangers to you
5. There are weapons involved

QUESTION 2: EVEN IF YOU ARE SAFE, WILL YOU BE BREAKING THE VIOLENCE LADDER?

If not – don't intervene – call the police or school staff.

When you intervene:

1. Never use violence to solve the problem
2. Never react emotionally

10 Things

We Can All Do
To Reduce The Number
Of Offenders

1. **TEACH CHILDREN TO BE INDIVIDUALS AND MAKE SMART CHOICES**

2. **TEACH KIDS THE CONSEQUENCES OF VIOLENCE**

3. **PLAN AND MONITOR TV WATCHING**

4. **SET FIRM BOUNDARIES FOR CHILDREN AND ENFORCE THEM**

5. **BE A GOOD ROLE MODEL FOR YOUR KIDS**

6. **TEACH KIDS GOOD VALUES AT AN EARLY AGE**

7. **BUILD HIGH SELF-ESTEEM**

8. **CHALLENGE YOUR KIDS AND LEARN ABOUT THEIR LIFE**

9. **GIVE YOUR KIDS THE ATTENTION THEY NEED**

10. **LEARN ALL YOU CAN ABOUT THE WORLD OUR CHILDREN LIVE IN**

12

AN EXAMPLE OF TEAMWORK

I walked out in front of the classroom and the March meeting got underway. "As you probably all realize, tonight is our last meeting together." There were assorted cheers and groans from the parents in front of me. "We've covered a lot of ground this year and now we just have one more topic to look at. Back at the beginning of the year we established there are three points we need to understand in order to protect our children from youth violence. In the first couple of meetings we spent some time looking at the first of those points – the world our children are growing up in today is very different from the one we knew as kids. Then we moved on to consider the Violence Ladder and how small tensions – if left unresolved – can escalate into serious crime. That was the second of the three points and, in the course of examining the Violence Ladder, we talked about gangs and also tried to understand the extent of the youth violence problem using statistics.

"Since January, though, we've been talking about how parents can help protect their kids. So far, we've managed to come up with a comprehensive list of behaviours that may indicate that your child is a victim of youth violence, and we've discussed concrete things that you can do in your own home to protect your children. Also, we've looked at how you can help reduce the number of offenders in your neighbourhood.

"Now there is only one more major subject left to cover – 'The Prevention Triangle: how parents, schools and police can work together to reduce youth violence.' Before we begin our discussion, however, I have a story that illustrates how The Prevention Triangle works.

PETER'S STORY

"In the past month, I've been working closely with the students and staff at a high school downtown. Prior to this year the school had never really had any serious problems with vandalism or youth violence. But, since September, graffiti had been springing up on the walls. In the beginning, the school staff hadn't thought the problem was very serious. Only a few small, spray-painted symbols had appeared on the walls near the entrance to the gym. The caretakers had been able to paint over the marks, and, although they hadn't been able to determine who was doing it, the principal, Mr. MacFarlane, felt they had the situation under control.

"However, as the year wore on, the tagging problem worsened. The tags started appearing more and more frequently. They become larger and more intricate. Recently, the graffiti had evolved into more elaborate pictures and swirling designs. Now the graffiti was being sprayed so frequently that the caretakers and school staff were having a hard time keeping the walls clean. At that point, Mr. MacFarlane called me. He was concerned the other kids would join in when they saw the original taggers getting away with it. The teachers were even afraid that the graffiti meant gangs were moving into their school. They worried that the outside of the school would soon be covered in overlapping spray-paint symbols and that violence or turf wars between gangs would follow.

"In response to Mr. MacFarlane's call, I went out to the school to take a look at the graffiti and speak with some of the students. I arrived at the school early on a Tuesday morning and went to the principal's office to check in. It was a fairly new high school, built in the '80s. There was lots of glass, the place was very bright and the halls were wide and clean. It wasn't like the dark, small, and kind of grim schools a lot of us went to as kids which were probably built just after the war. This school even had a large common area where the kids could hang out between classes. On my way to the office I walked through it, looking at the kids lounging around. I wasn't surprised to find that they were fairly typical – broken off into small groups of friends, each clique a little different from the one beside it. There were grunge, preppy, gothic and skaters; name a subculture and it was represented. But nobody was causing any trouble, these were just regular kids hanging out at lunch. However, as I walked by the risers the kids were sitting on, I did notice something that disturbed me. Although the rest of the room was neat and relatively clean, I saw a small line of graffiti along one of the risers. And, when I bent over to check it out, I was stunned because I recognized the tag.

"About two months prior to my visit I'd given a warning to a 15-year-old kid named Peter who'd been spraying his tag across the back wall of a store in the area. I knew he wasn't a member of any gang, because the tag that I'd caught him painting wasn't a recognized gang symbol. He claimed he just loved spray art. Either way, I'd scared him half to death that day, by threatening to arrest him for vandalism. But it seemed like he just hadn't been able to stop. On the riser in front of me a long row of identical symbols was painted onto the wood – it was that same crucifix and radiation symbol.

"In the principal's office a few minutes later, I explained what I had seen and Mr. MacFarlane was able to confirm that the graffiti they were finding on the school walls was similar. When I asked him if he had a student named Peter, who would be in grade ten, Mr. MacFarlane knew immediately who I was talking about. But I was surprised to hear that Peter was well-known to everyone in the school as an athlete. I was expecting Peter to have been recognizable to the principal because he had been in and out of trouble, not because he was a good basketball player. Mr. MacFarlane had trouble believing that Peter might be the one responsible for the graffiti. I asked him to call Peter down to the office so that I could speak with him.

"I waited for him in an empty classroom near the office while the principal went to pull Peter out of a math class. When Peter came into the room he recognized me immediately.

"'Hello, Peter, how are ya?' I asked, gesturing towards the empty chair in front of the teacher's desk where I sat.

"He shuffled his frame into the chair, looked nervously at the principal and straightened his posture. 'Uh, hi, sir,' he said, his voice a little shaky. Mr. MacFarlane nodded at me and then closed the door behind him on his way out.

"'Do you know why Mr. MacFarlane brought you down to speak to me today, Peter?' I asked. Peter shook his head silently. 'Recently we've had a problem with graffiti on some of the outside walls of the school,' I continued. 'Since the beginning of the school year kids have been spray-painting tags on the side of the building, and this morning I found the same tags on the bleachers in the common area. Have you seen the stuff

I'm talking about?' While I was talking I looked directly into Peter's eyes, but he was looking down, staring at the black-and-white tile floor.

"I decided to wait until he answered before going on. A few uncomfortable seconds passed and then, finally, Peter stammered, 'Yeah, yeah I guess I've seen some stuff on the school. I didn't do it though. I swear! I haven't done any tagging since you gave me the warning, honest.' His eyes were darting all over the place.

"'Peter, how stupid do I look?' I asked, 'Don't you think I remember what your tag looks like? It's a red radiation symbol.'

"He swallowed hard. 'Yeah, I used to use that, but maybe somebody else was just copying it,' he said, looking nervously over at the door.

"'People usually look away when they lie. You've been staring a hole in that door over there ever since I started asking you questions. Come on Peter, level with me, you're the one who's been spraying the school aren't you?'

"Peter looked down at his feet. His breath became very irregular. I waited for him to say something.

"'Yeah. . .' he said.

"'Yeah?' I asked.

"'Yeah, it was me who's been tagging the school,' he said, looking up at me, his speech getting faster. 'I just did a little at first, but nobody around here did anything about it, except paint over it once in awhile. I just like to paint, you know. I can't afford canvas. The walls are so big and everyone sees it. All the other guys know me 'cause I do those tags. I slowed down, stopped for awhile after you caught me. But – I don't know – I just started again I guess.'

"'Peter,' I said, leaning forward towards him. 'When we talked last time what did I say to you?'

"'Uh, like, tagging is illegal,' he said, 'You said it's like vandalism. But, I stopped painting on that guy's wall. I. . .' he began stammering, 'Are you going to charge me?'

"'It's not like vandalism, Peter. It is vandalism. It is a crime. And yes you probably will be charged,' I replied. I tried not to let it show, but I was angry at this kid for being so stupid. I'd only given him a warning two months ago and now I would have to take him to the station and process him with all the other criminals.

"Peter panicked, his eyes became really wide and he choked on his voice. 'No,' he said, 'I can't. . . . Please, give me another chance. I won't do it again. I didn't hurt anyone. I can't go to jail.' I could see from the sudden change in expression on Peter's face that the thought of going to jail terrified him. He obviously wasn't used to dealing with cops and that was a good sign. This was no hardened criminal, no chronic young offender who'd spent most of his teenage years in youth court or detention. But the question remained – why start breaking the law now?

"'Well, jail's not likely,' I said, 'but, if I take you down to the station, a criminal record is. I'm not giving you a break, Peter. The warning that I gave you last time was exactly that. And if your problem goes unaddressed here, then the warning becomes meaningless. We're going to call your parents–'

"'My parents?!'

"'– both of them. And get them in here to talk with me and Mr. MacFarlane and you. Together we're going to come to an agreement about how to solve this problem. . . .'

"'No, my parents will kill me!'

"'– criminal charges are still very possible.'

He looked down again. 'Okay,' he said, realizing that he had little choice.

"An hour later we were all sitting around Mr. MacFarlane's desk in his office – Peter, Mr. MacFarlane, myself and Peter's parents, Joe and Karen. When I introduced myself they both said hello, and smiled, shaking my hand. But, they seemed nervous, just like their son had been an hour before. I often have to remind myself when I make these types of calls that these people probably don't come into contact with the police very often. And the possibility that their son might be in serious criminal trouble is one of the scariest things that a parent has to face. In fact, that's why I try to involve parents as much as I can, whenever I make an arrest. It helps them to understand what their child has done and why the police are proceeding to arrest. It means that parents and police aren't divided over the child.

"'Do you know why Peter is in trouble at school, and do you realize why I'm here speaking to you today?' I asked.

"Joe looked sheepish and sort of embarrassed, 'Well, yes,' he said. 'Peter was caught vandalizing school property and, from what Mr. MacFarlane said, you're considering pressing criminal charges.'

"Before he could continue or I could reply, Karen jumped in, 'But, Officer Guest, what's going to happen to Peter? He's just a boy. He's not going to jail is he? I don't want him to have a record. It was just a kid's prank that got out of control. . . .'

"'Well, that's actually why I'm here. No, I don't think that Peter will be charged, not if we can come up with a solution to this problem together,' I said. 'But, as Mr. MacFarlane may have told you, I've already been involved with Peter in a case of vandalism before. In that instance I issued him a warning and didn't expect to have to deal with him again for the same thing.'

"'Peter didn't actually hurt anybody. But, what he did is against the law. It created added work, expense and frustration for the school staff and eventually it could have led to larger problems with gangs. Defacing school or any other property is a crime and should be punished as such.'

"'So, what do we do now?' asked Joe.

"'Well, Mr. MacFarlane has advised me that the school doesn't want to press charges. But this is a partnership so I'd like to hear what else you think should be done,' I said.

"Joe looked at his son and asked, 'Why? Why would you do something like this? Look at all the trouble you caused for yourself and us and the school.'

"Peter looked up and swallowed hard. 'I don't know,' he began, 'I guess I was just bored. I wasn't really enjoying basketball, and, I dunno – I like painting and stuff. That's what I want to do.'

"'Oh, Peter,' said his mother, 'you should have come to us. We could have done something, maybe bought you an easel and some supplies or something.' She shook her head and reached out to her son.

"'Officer Guest, we really had no idea about Peter's behaviour before now,' she said. 'Frankly we're shocked and, to tell you the truth, embarrassed.'

"'I think Peter needs to be punished,' said Joe. 'But I don't want him to go to jail. He'll definitely be grounded and lose privileges at home – and I'm sure Mr. MacFarlane has some input as well.'

"'Well, the school will have to discipline Peter,' said Mr. MacFarlane. 'I'm sorry, Joe and Karen, but what Peter has done is very serious and can't be left unaddressed. That would send the wrong message to the other students and to the staff. We don't want students and teachers thinking that crime is okay and that we don't have mechanisms for dealing with it. I'm going to recommend a suspension, probably three days. And, also, I think Peter should be involved in cleaning-up the walls. After school he will serve detention and will repaint the areas of the school he has defaced.' I glanced over at Peter – he looked terrible. He knew the next few weeks were not going to be easy.

"'Okay, sounds like we have an agreement,' I said. 'But there are a couple of things I think we should consider before we're finished here.'

"'Like what?' asked Joe.

"'Well, I'm going to commit to following up with you and Peter over the next few months. Whenever I'm in this school I'll check with Mr. MacFarlane on his progress. As well, I'd suggest that the guidance counselor here at the school get involved.'

"'I agree,' Mr. MacFarlane said, 'I'll have Mr. Gerulitis talk to you, Peter. I think you two should meet on a regular basis.'

"Peter nodded and looked over at his parents to see how they were taking it. In a low voice he said, 'I'm really sorry about what I did. I guess I didn't really think it was a big deal, but it was illegal.'

"Karen put her hand on her son's shoulder. 'Do you have any suggestions for us, Officer Guest? What can we do?'

"'Basically and most importantly, you have to get interested — show some enthusiasm for what he's doing,' I told her. 'Take even just an hour each day to talk to him. I'll tell you the same things I tell all the parents – talk to your kid, ask questions and then really listen hard to what he tells you in return. Then act on that knowledge. Ask him about his friends, where he goes, what he does, what he wants to do, what he's interested in, what he likes and doesn't like at school. I'd sign him up for some courses. Find another outlet for his art, rather than having him plaster his work all over somebody else's wall. Give him a place to paint and make sure it's set up so that he doesn't wreck the place and drive you guys crazy.'

"We all left that meeting on a relatively positive note – it could have been much worse. In the end, Peter was suspended, his parents grounded him and I think he was scared straight. I've kept in touch over the past few months and, so far, there haven't been any more problems. I know that Joe and Karen are much more involved in what their son is doing. Peter is meeting with Mr. Gerulitis, the guidance counselor. In this case, the situation was handled very well."

13

THE PREVENTION TRIANGLE: HOW PARENTS, SCHOOLS AND POLICE CAN WORK TOGETHER

"Okay," I said, "I'd like to use Peter's story as a lead into something I call the Prevention Triangle – how parents and schools and police can work together to reduce youth violence.

TEAMWORK BETWEEN PARENTS, SCHOOLS AND POLICE

"As Peter's story shows, the key to building safe schools is teamwork between parents, school staff and community organizations such as the police. When Peter's school realized that they had a tagging problem on their hands they initially tried to deal with it on their own. If you remember, they had been finding spray-painted logos on the walls since September, but for months all they did was paint over them and hope that the problem went away. They didn't tell anybody they had a problem and they didn't ask for any help."

I looked around at all the parents. "Does that remind anybody of anything we've discussed in earlier meetings?" I asked.

Mary put up her hand. "Yeah," she said, trying to remember, "it sounds sort of like that first story we heard — the one where the kid was harassed by the group of bullies who wanted him to buy a knife. He didn't buy it and they continued to threaten him and eventually he got beaten up. But that never would have happened if he had told his parents or reported what was happening to a teacher or the principal. This situation with Peter sounds kinda the same. If the school had reported their problem to the police earlier, then the problem could have been solved much more quickly."

"Yes, that was Rick and Jamie's story that you're talking about, and you're right – the situations are the same. Also, we saw the same thing in the story where George confronted a group of kids who had stolen his son's bike and was assaulted. He should not have tried to handle that situation alone. He should have called the police. Just like the school in Peter's story, George didn't call for help. We've already talked a lot about the importance of communication in breaking the Violence Ladder. We've said that parents, children, schools and police need to work as a team to prevent kids from becoming victims and reduce the number of offenders. And that means not only should our children report harassment or threats, but schools and parents also need to report criminal infractions to the police as well.

THE PREVENTION TRIANGLE

"In order to break the Violence Ladder we need to communicate," I said, walking to the blackboard and picking up a piece of a chalk. "Think of the people involved as forming the sharp points or corners of a triangle," I continued, drawing a triangle on the board with the chalk. "Parents on one corner, schools on another and police on the third. The sides of the triangle represent the partnerships that are formed between police, parents and schools. You can even think of the kids as inside that triangle for their protection. If we are all involved then the structure is solid – the necessary resources for fighting violence are represented by this triangle. If we act alone, there's no triangle, only a single point – and we're more likely to fail that way.

"In Peter's case you can see how important it was for the school to get me involved. I had more experience with kids who tag and, luckily, I was able to recognize the tag and help them to stop Peter. That shows how important teamwork between schools and police is, but even still, the Prevention Triangle must be completed – parents must become intimately involved in all aspects of any case involving their children.

3 STEPS TO CREATING THE PREVENTION TRIANGLE BETWEEN PARENTS, SCHOOLS AND POLICE

"In order to create the Prevention Triangle we need teamwork between parents, schools and police. And that requires three simple things from all of us: we must be informed, we must communicate, and we must always be consistent.

WE MUST BE INFORMED

"Parents, educators, and police must be informed about school policies and programs, and about the law. This will ensure that we all react properly to any breach of policies or transgression of the law. There are many different programs run by schools and police departments across the country. A complete description of them is slightly beyond the scope of this meeting. But I would certainly be able to come back and tell you all about them at a future parents association meeting.

WE MUST COMMUNICATE

"We've already talked about how communication helps create the triangle. Communication ensures that the right people are doing their job. Nobody is kept out of the loop. But communication doesn't mean communicating only when an incident occurs – it means communication on an ongoing basis, especially between the parents and schools. Parents should be talking to their child's teachers, as well as other school staff, such as the attendance VP, or guidance counselor. This way parents know about their child's marks, their absences, their attitude at school, the choice of friends, and any sudden changes in extracurricular involvement. This will help everybody recognize some of the warning signs of being a victim that we discussed a few months ago. Remember, something like a rash of absences can indicate that a child is afraid of something at school.

"And of course, parents and educators need to communicate with the police on a regular basis or as soon as any police issues arise. Police can help parents and teachers be aware of youth violence problems outside the school and in the neighbourhood – problems that affect everybody.

WE MUST ALWAYS BE CONSISTENT

"Consistency is something that is only possible once the first two points – being informed and communication – are in place. Once we know what we are all doing, as well as what we should be doing according to policies and laws, then we must make the effort to be consistent. I think this is crucial – conflicting messages only serve to confuse kids and generate the perception that adults don't know what they're doing, can't help, or aren't interested. If we don't have a uniform reaction to a problem, the prevention triangle breaks down.

"In fact, the kids themselves have told us they rely heavily on schools and parents to be consistent in their response to youth violence. If a kid is arrested for assault on another student, and his or her parents were to claim that the police were making up the charges or the school didn't see fit to suspend or punish the offender, then both victim and offender lose. The victim will believe that reporting violent incidents doesn't help and will probably never report one again – even if they are threatened or beaten. The offender will see that the consequences that should have followed from his criminal behaviour were not carried out, and he or she is more likely to commit an offense again.

LACK OF CONSISTENCY CAN BE COSTLY

"Here's another example of what can go wrong when we are inconsistent. In this case, the school staff didn't react as a unit to a very serious problem.

"Not too long ago, a teacher in an Ontario high school was assaulted by a 15-year-old student while he was escorting that student to the principal's office. The kid surprised him with a punch to the chest and, when he stumbled, the student pushed him down and started kicking and punching him. The kid had to be pulled off by three other staff. He bit a caretaker, puncturing the skin. The teacher needed nine stitches and missed a lot of work, but the most hideous and frightening part of this story is that the teacher became the butt of jokes from other teachers. He was never asked if he was okay, and the entire incident was just treated like a joke, and that to me is unacceptable. I know that's an extreme case but I think it's a fairly good indicator of where things will end up if we don't take these problems in our schools seriously.

"The solution is consistency. We need to define which behaviours for students are acceptable and which are unacceptable, and then make everyone aware that we will enforce consistent disciplinary procedures that reflect a zero-tolerance attitude towards violence. The disciplinary procedures must be applied uniformly across the entire student body. They must also balance the rights of victims to live and work in a safe environment with the rights of the offender to receive an education and have access to support and resources. When the situation calls for punishment or police involvement, it must be forthcoming. In the case of the teacher who was beaten, I think the school let him down and did a very poor job of dealing with the student. That offender received the message that violence doesn't have severe consequences.

THE PREVENTION TRIANGLE IN ACTION

"I make a point of practicing the Prevention Triangle. That's why, when dealing with Peter, I called his parents, Joe and Karen. We could have just charged Peter with vandalism and given him a court date. It's very likely that his parents wouldn't have found out about their son's problem until they received a phone call from the police. I don't believe that's the best way to handle most situations. Just think how you would feel about your son and about the police if that happened to you?"

"I'd be furious at my son if I got a call like that," said Mary.

"I'm sure you would," I replied, "so would most parents. But I see a lot of confrontation between parents of kids who are arrested and the police. In many cases, the call from the police station is indeed the first time parents hear that their child is in any trouble. And when they get to the station, most parents are in shock. They don't want to believe their child could have committed a crime. The fact that they now find themselves in a police station after their child has been arrested makes them react even more strongly than they otherwise might have. They were not involved in the process at any time and are now faced with only two choices: they either believe their child, or the arresting officer. Although both parents and police are trying to prevent kids from becoming victims and reduce the number of offenders, this situation often divides us. If the parents choose to side with their child it's as though the police or schools have said, 'You're a lawbreaker, we're the peacekeepers. You're bad and we're good.' I think that's hard for parents to handle, so they need input into what happens with their child.

"I'm not saying we shouldn't arrest kids, but I think Peter's story shows there is often a more effective way to deal with problem situations. I called his parents immediately and informed everyone – the parents, Peter, and Mr. MacFarlane – that we should come up with a workable solution together, even if it does involve arrest. I think parents should be heavily involved in this step because they will be helping to make the community safe.

"Although parents don't have input into whether or not an arrest is made, the fact that Peter's parents were involved in the process of disciplining him made them feel like they were partners with the school and police department. They were able to find out why he did what he did, and we all made sure the punishment was appropriate and that there would be a follow-up with Peter. The school promised to watch him closely and made him clean up what he had done. In the end, he was suspended, but no charges were laid. Perhaps most importantly, his parents found out about Peter's commitment to art, and now they are able to encourage him and to make sure he has more outlets for his creative energy.

"Peter's story shows how I got the parents involved. But it works the other way too. Please make sure you get the school and the police involved whenever something arises. If your child comes home complaining that another student is threatening them, don't hesitate to call the school – and make sure they take it seriously. A lot of schools now have a police officer they call on regularly, and, in many cases, the officer is familiar with the school staff and some of the students. This familiarity is a great asset in dealing with problems, officers may already know who the culprit is and how best to deal with him or her.

SUMMARY

"Well, I've covered all of the points that I wanted to. We discussed the Prevention Triangle that is formed by the partnership among parents, police and schools. Also, we saw that in order to create the Prevention Triangle, we need to do three things: one – we must be informed; two – we must communicate; and three – we must always be consistent. If we can do these three things, then we will effectively protect our kids.

167

OVERALL SUMMARY

"Since this is the end of this series of meetings, I think it would be a good idea to take a few minutes to review what we've learned. As you know, my goal was to make protecting your children from youth violence as simple as possible, and to give you some concrete solutions that you can use in your own homes right away. That's why we came up with the 3 most important points to understand about youth violence. Let's look at them in order.

"Firstly, we learned that the pressures facing our children are very different and much more intense than the ones we felt when we were their age. They live in a world where violence is common.

"Secondly, we learned that violence is often the result of a series of incidents that escalates in severity from harassment to threats, to grouping, to weapons, and then to violence. So, breaking the Violence Ladder should be our number one priority.

"Thirdly, we learned that there are things parents can do to protect their kids. We discussed the 19 warning signs that indicate your kid might be a victim of youth violence, 13 things you can do at home to protect your kids, and 10 ways to reduce the number of offenders. We also examined how to protect our kids using the Prevention Triangle formed by parents, police and schools.

"Thanks, once again, for listening and for your valuable input. I know that our children will benefit from the time we have spent together. If all parents, everywhere, were to look for warning signs, work towards breaking the Violence Ladder and truly communicate with their children, we would see a dramatic difference in our society. As you know, there are articles on youth violence in the newspaper on a daily basis, and I'd like to see that stop. So please do your part. Our children will shape tomorrow's society, and when I'm 65 I don't want everybody to live in fear – surrounded by threat and violence and disorder."

3 STEPS TO CREATING THE PREVENTION TRIANGLE BETWEEN PARENTS, SCHOOLS AND POLICE

1. We must be informed

2. We must communicate

3. We must always be consistent.

EPILOGUE

We must communicate

I urge you all to take action against the problem of youth violence. It will not go away on its own, so parents, children, educators and police must talk to each other. If your child comes home with suspicious bruises, find out why – call the school, call the police. If you hear of gangs or weapons, harassment or threats in your child's school or neighbourhood, call someone.

I hope, after reading Youth Violence: How To Protect Your Kids, you feel empowered to help reduce youth violence. You should now have some tools to help you protect your kids at home as well as understand the many ways you can help out in your schools and communities.

Most importantly, we must all work hard to stay close to our kids, and somehow we must give guidance to other parents who need it, because good parenting is the best solution for combating youth violence. Being proactive with children at an early age goes a lot further towards curbing aggressive behaviour than sending a young teenage offender to a correctional facility.

I will continue learning all I can about how to prevent youth violence – you should too. And, as always, talking to parents and kids will always be a big part of my life.

APPENDIX

APPENDIX

What schools are doing to reduce youth violence

A couple weeks after our last meeting, I got a call from John, the principal, to come and hold a special meeting about what is being done in the schools to solve the problem of youth violence.

When I got up in front of the parents again, I started off by saying, "Tonight we'll discuss the various programs and approaches that schools use to tackle youth violence. However, I'd like to begin by discussing how the kids think the schools should handle youth violence. Then I'd like to divide our discussion into two sections. In the first section we'll focus on the reactive approaches and programs in the schools. In the second section we'll focus on the preventative approach.

WHAT KIDS THINK SHOULD BE DONE IN THE SCHOOLS

"I've already mentioned that kids want consistency from us. But more fundamentally, they want us to get involved. They want their parents to get involved and they want police and educators to play both proactive and reactive roles in reducing group and gang-based crime in the schools – especially violence. In effect, the kids want to see the Prevention Triangle.

WHAT SCHOOL STAFF CAN DO OUTSIDE OF GOVERNMENT-SPONSORED PROGRAMS

"According to the students, in order to control the problem of violence, educators need to be aware of what is going on in their classrooms, in their hallways, the parking lots and in the streets around their schools.

"I'm glad to say that teachers and principals have begun to monitor their school grounds more carefully. Schools are now making changes to areas where they have experienced ongoing problems. In some cases this means installing lights, or even cameras, or giving walkie-talkies to the staff so they are in constant communication with the office. Many of the worst areas are being monitored by staff or professional hall monitors at critical times.

"As well, school administrators, from trustee to vice-principal, are doing a much better job of learning what goes on in their schools by talking to staff.

"If the school staff do a good job of staying on top of what is happening in their hallways, school yards and parking lots, they can be an excellent source of information for parents and police. As parents you can then ask schools for frequent and accurate reporting of the crime and violence in the school. It'll help you to be aware of what your child is facing everyday at school and what issues you need to deal with immediately."

SECTION 1: REACTING TO YOUTH VIOLENCE IN THE SCHOOLS

Robert raised his hand and asked, "I'm sorry if I'm being impatient here and jumping ahead a bit, but what exactly are the schools doing to protect my kid from the weapons that we hear about in schools? All the time in the news I hear about knives and guns making their way into our schools and how all the kids have them. You told us about weapons use in our schools and the school board always gives us updates on the seriousness of the problem in our district. They tell us how many weapons have been confiscated – stuff like that. So what are the schools doing about weapons?"

"Well, thanks, Robert," I said. "This actually leads us into our discussion of policies and programs.

"I think John might actually be able to get us started on this one. John why don't you tell us what measures you have in place right here at this school?" I said and looked over in his direction.

John stood up, cleared his throat and addressed the parents. "Well, a lot of these things you may already be aware of, if you've been talking to your kids. We have locker searches, ID badges, parking stickers for school parking lots, and policies on student conduct, violence and weapons use. Some schools don't allow pagers, cell phones, baseball caps, or team jackets on their property."

WHAT IS ZERO TOLERANCE AGAINST VIOLENCE?

"And what exactly is zero tolerance?" Robert asked. "Does that mean that if a kid hits another kid he goes to jail? Does it mean they are thrown out of school and never let back in?

"Well, not always, Robert," John replied. "We do have an obligation – a legal one – to give a kid seven years of schooling regardless of what they do."

Robert was furious, "What? C'mon. That's the problem with all of these programs. I mean just talking to these kids isn't going help, is it? If they're carrying guns and robbing other kids as you say, then a stern lecture from the vice principal isn't going to make them stop, is it? If we don't arrest them, then doesn't that send a message to the kids that violence is tolerated?"

"Well, you really have to judge each situation independently and that's why we have so many different programs in our schools." John said. "But I understand your frustration, and so do the schools. What we have now in many school districts around the country is a zero-tolerance policy. Zero tolerance in plain English means we won't put up with violence of any kind in our schools and each time a violent act is carried out we will respond. For every inappropriate behaviour there will be an appropriate response or consequence. Zero tolerance is a media invention. Those words were actually only mentioned a couple of times in the Scarborough Board of Education's 'Safe Schools Policy.' It is not just concerned with expelling offenders, but outlines a wide range of responses. Essentially, what it looks like is a written set of guidelines for teachers, staff and students outlining the boundaries of acceptable student behaviour. What's especially important is that those guidelines also include the repercussions for stepping outside those bounds. At it's core, zero tolerance is an attempt to take violence out of our schools by saying these violent and criminal behaviours are unacceptable. It says to students that just because they are students they are not exempt from legal action.

"Underlying zero tolerance are a few key ideas that came out of a lot of recent research into the causes of youth violence. Those studies stated that violence is a broad cultural problem and needs the cooperation of parents, police and school staff to be dealt with. They showed that we need to directly and openly confront criminal behaviour in the schools and that means we need to establish formal policies for dealing with students. Underlining those policies is the idea that the welfare of the majority of the students, our sons and daughters who are in school to learn, not to commit crimes, should take precedence over the welfare of the few troublemakers. Basically, both students and their parents must be held accountable for their behaviour."

"So how does that work, John?" Robert asked. "What about when my son tells me teachers are being beaten up for getting involved? Kevin just told us that story about the teacher who needed stitches. And I heard that one teacher in a school about a mile from here was beaten with a lead pipe because he tried to break up a fight in one of his classrooms. They actually came back later and beat him."

I took the floor from John at this point. "I've talked to teachers myself and in many situations those teachers were afraid to confront kids in their classrooms, in the hallways or in the school yard. Without support and a framework like zero tolerance, there was no way they would step in and try to break up a fight, for exactly those reasons you just cited. So we need to be firm, establish boundaries for our kids at school and stick to them. That's what zero tolerance is all about. At school, in cases like those you mentioned, where there has been a clear violation of school policy or the law, we will respond appropriately.

"We know that zero tolerance works. Where it has been implemented, weapons use has dropped by two thirds, which is an amazing impact. So, I would even suggest that we begin sending the message to younger students that violence won't be tolerated. We need to speak to elementary school students and convince them that crime isn't an option before they are tempted by weapons or other negative influences."

As I finished Mary asked, "Okay, maybe zero tolerance has worked, but the way you and John are describing it still worries me. I mean, if we expel, suspend or throw the offenders in jail, aren't we just creating a bigger problem for ourselves? They will have missed their education and won't they just end up on the streets committing crimes?"

"Well that would be true if we didn't have other programs and solutions," I answered. "Even with zero tolerance we still believe kids are entitled to an education. And because school staff, police and parents all firmly believe that, we always look at each case individually to see if there are any alternatives to jail or expulsion. There are many good examples of programs that take students who have over-stepped the bounds of the zero tolerance policy, and try to rehabilitate them, with the hope of eventually returning them to a regular school program without further incident.

TAKING THE OFFENDER OUT OF THE CLASSROOM

"A friend of mine, Stu Auty, who is the head of the Canadian Safe School Task Force, believes that there are a lot of programs that work.

"Stu is a big believer in programs that get the kids out of their environment – which he calls their power center and their power structure – and put them in a different environment. Basically what he's talking about are programs that take kids from urban settings or depressed neighbourhoods and give them a new experience – hopefully giving them a new perspective. For instance, with the backing of the Ontario Institute for Secondary Education, Stu put together a group which takes high-risk kids who could easily become chronic young offenders to an outdoor site near Hamilton for 5 days. It's an outdoor, adventure-based program. And, according to Stu, it has had tremendous results.

"When the kids are out there, they learn about responsibility, bonding, rules, and regulations. They are taken to a picturesque site with rivers, forests, and rock gorges, where they rock climb, learn to cross rope bridges and do other things they never could in the city. All this helps them develop self-esteem. They learn to depend on one another, work as a group and succeed as a team. They learn interdependence and come back with a sense of pride. I've seen some of the kids both before and after they went on the program and it's surprising how much it affects them.

"The Bark Lake program is very similar to Stu's program. Kids who are at risk of becoming serious offenders are taken from their school or neighbourhood and sent to the Bark Lake Center. This is a wilderness site, right in the middle of Ontario's cottage country. Once they're up there, the kids are taught teamwork and leadership skills, and encouraged to test themselves in challenging outdoor activities, such as rope climbing. A huge percentage of the students who agree to participate in that program agree that they were changed for the better by the experience.

DIFFERENT SCHOOLS FOR HARD-CORE OFFENDERS OR HIGH-RISK KIDS

"There's a program in Buffalo, New York, for instance that Stu has been studying for the longest time. In fact, he's trying to bring it here to

Ontario. That program is one where they don't put kids in a natural setting, but take them out of their classroom and put them into an alternative school setting. In the new setting the ratio of teachers to students is very high, so the kids get a high level of specialized attention. They are constantly watched and counseled. Their positive behaviour is reinforced and negative behaviour is immediately dealt with. And they can't go back to their regular school setting until they straighten out. They've got about an 80% success rating.

BOOT CAMPS FOR YOUNG OFFENDERS

"They are not schools, but boot camps are very topical, so I'd like to talk about them for a moment. The United States has programs in place in which hard-core offenders are put to work in orange coveralls as part of old-fashioned chain gangs. Instead of passing time in jail they work for the county – splitting rocks or logging. Near Red Deer, Alberta, we actually have our own version of the boot camp where violent kids clear land for the construction of a new oil drilling rig. Near the town of Nordegg, convicted repeat offenders work at hard manual labour, as well as physical fitness and learning programs. This camp has been around for at least two years, but in recent months the idea of boot camps has become a hotly debated issue in newspapers all over the country.

"People have divided opinions about boot camps for several reasons. Some see the creation of these camps as a political strategy to gain votes. Others protest the cruel conditions that the youth are forced to work under, drawing parallels to Siberian labour camps and the racist stigma of the American chain gang. However, a significant percentage of the population see them as great opportunities for reforming hardened young criminals before they reach the adult justice system. Many people feel that programs, such as the one in place at Nordegg, ease the load on our overburdened jails and they applaud the tough stance that politicians appear to be taking with young offenders.

"A typical day at Nordegg begins at 6 AM. and ends 15 and a half brutal hours later at 9:30 PM. In addition to clearing forests, the kids must attend life skills courses which attempt to teach them the rudimentary skills they will need for a successful life outside of jail. They learn budgeting, resume writing and interview skills. The hard work under terrible conditions is necessary to teach the kids discipline. All of this is part of the underlying philosophy behind the boot camps. It is hoped that serious young offenders who have some desire to reform will benefit by being removed from the environment where they committed their crimes, much like the last two types of programs that I mentioned. In fact, the early results are encouraging. In the first year and a half, only 15 of the 140 graduates had gone on to commit another crime after leaving the camp.

THE ALTERNATIVE CURRICULUM FOR EDUCATING STUDENTS

"In New Brunswick, there is also an Alternative Curriculum for Educating Students. Students who are in danger of leaving or being thrown out of school can enroll at the ACES school and will be given a study program specifically designed to fit their unique needs. There are generally no more than ten kids for every one teacher, and students spend as much time as is necessary at this school before being returned to their original school.

"Those types of programs have two big benefits. First, they remove the bad influence from a teacher's classroom. And that's important because now the teacher can actually concentrate on his or her job. Instead of taking time out of every class to discipline or otherwise deal with bad kids, a teacher can actually teach. And second, the student is removed to a distant setting where they can improve. If they don't, they don't go back to their friends. The key there is that the kid is not surrounded by their friends, so peer pressure doesn't influence their behaviour. As we saw before Christmas, popularity and support from friends are both strong factors in gang formation, so separation is crucial.

POSITIVE PEER GROUPS

"We know from all of our research that a positive peer group can actually help prior offenders learn acceptable behaviours and the values that encourage those behaviours – like trust and responsibility. So programs that mix high-risk students with a large group of high-achieving kids can actually alter the high-risk student's behaviour – straighten them out, as it were. In the same way, giving a high-risk kid the chance to excel or to be challenged by something they are really interested in, or something they enjoy is also a good way for educators to jump-start a kid. Parents who feel that their child is slipping – beginning to wander down a path towards delinquency – should suggest that he or she is enrolled in something like that. It can be as specific as Stu's program or as common as joining the basketball team, but it gives them a purpose, a positive peer group, and a challenge. It teaches them teamwork, perseverance, and gives them some positive reinforcement. For the first time, many of them find themselves being congratulated for their behaviour on school property instead of being challenged and punished. That can make all the difference.

INVOLVE STUDENTS

"Another type of program that has been very effective at dealing with youth violence in our schools are those actually administered by students themselves.

"Personally, I feel it would be ideal if all students were encouraged in every possible way to take ownership and responsibility for the safety and security of their schools. School staff should encourage their students to organize a school-watch program or school-safety committee that allows kids to anonymously report potential or actual crime to the staff. Such programs can also be used together with police action to catch kids who threaten school safety or to prevent potentially dangerous situations before they escalate.

PEER MEDIATION

"Along those lines there is a very successful program operating right now in a number of Canadian and American schools called Peer Mediation. The principle behind it is simple: kids learn intervention strategies and effective ways of coping with stress and are taught how to step in-between other students who have a conflict and help them resolve it. The kids themselves solve the problem. Somewhat surprisingly, they think it's a very effective way of reducing the threat in their schools. The biggest advantage is that it gives the two parties a way to save face in front of their friends. The mediation takes place inside a closed room, between the two agitators and one or two mediators. And it is often used as an alternative to detention or suspension for the kids involved. If the mediation works – and it usually does – the students leave the room feeling that they have solved a problem and their friends don't see them as having chickened out of a fight. I've spoken to some of the twenty or thirty students who are trained as mediators in each school every year, and they appreciate and value the experience they get from it. They learn ways to communicate and resolve conflicts which can be invaluable later in life. That makes sense to me. I mean, think what a difference a program like that could make in this room, or in your workplace.

PEACEMAKERS

"As well as Peer Mediation, there's a program called Peacemakers, which is currently running in Ontario. It is similar to Peer Mediation, but for younger students. Each grade up to grade seven nominates peacemakers, whose role is to settle school-yard disputes on the spot using conflict resolution techniques.

"These programs could be set up here at this school, if you are interested or feel they are needed. They allow students to resolve conflicts safely and rationally as they arise, or contact the police when they have legitimate concerns about crime in their school. In schools where Peacemakers is practiced, the rate of violent or criminal incidents plummets. It really helps a lot of schools get the problem of school-yard bullying and harassment under control. And all of those things can be crucial at a time when budget cuts threaten to reduce the number of teachers and school staff who watch over our kids.

"In some schools, Peer Mediation and Peacemakers have been changed to allow for an entire court system in the school. Bullies actually stand trial in a school court run by students of their own age. These students actually run the process and even pass sentence on the bullies. As well, some schools have instigated a program in which the victims of bullies write letters to the offender telling them specifically how they felt, and what happened to them as a result of the assault or harassment.

"Again, as parents, you can encourage your school to set up such programs, or you can even jump right in and help out the school staff at times when there are large numbers of kids outside — like recess or lunch or before and after school. Usually bullying and harassment can be greatly reduced if there is adequate and interested supervision over the kids in the school yard and in the halls.

SECTION 2: PREVENTING YOUTH VIOLENCE IN THE SCHOOLS

PREVENTATIVE PROGRAMS AND COURSES

"As you can see, by teaching kids to coexist peacefully and letting them police each other, some of the programs I have just described can be effective in preventing youth violence. I think stuff like this is a great idea. We must give kids the skills they need to resolve conflicts. As well, we must educate them about each other to help eradicate tensions between different races or subcultures. We really need to put the power to reduce youth violence in the hands of the children and let them help themselves.

"I've heard from kids that an effective way for schools to do that is to deliver programs designed to get students from different cultural groups to work together. They teach kids about each others' cultures and teach them to be sensitive to the beliefs of their classmates. If we can provide opportunities for those kids to interact with each other, then schools can be successful in lowering the amount of conflict between students.

START EARLY

"A lot of the older students I talk to – the ones who are already offenders at 17 or 18 – tell me that they think that the problem is largely out of control by the time kids get into high school. That's why many of our existing programs, like zero tolerance and Crime Stoppers, are designed just to react to existing crime. Kids recognize the need to educate students and institute multicultural programs at very early ages. Young children should get used to making friends with kids from different cultures. Make it a non-issue. If these students get to know each other at an early age and then travel through school together it will cut down on the most dangerous conflicts when they hit high school.

THE HEALTHY RELATIONSHIPS PROGRAM

"The Healthy Relationships program in Nova Scotia, for instance, concentrates on violence prevention through the teaching of 'healthy relationship' courses to grade 7, 8 and 9 students. Again, they stress conflict management, gender equality and they try to get students to understand that clichés like 'men don't cry' or 'be a man' can lead to serious trouble.

HUMAN RELATIONS COURSES

"Human relations courses that cover similar ground are also being taught in many Ontario schools. I've actually been called in to speak to many classes and think they're very valuable. As one parent said to me, 'What kids need is someone to sit them down at an early age and tell them – straight out – what they should and shouldn't do. Give them life skills. Show them how to manage anger. Because I think a lot of kids aren't getting those skills at home.'

"There are different courses that have been created for teachers to use and there are also services and agencies that can be brought into schools to deal with anger management, stress management, sexuality, self-esteem, gang-proofing workshops and conflict resolution. Those all lead to better communication.

HOW THE SCHOOLS AND POLICE WORK TOGETHER

"The idea that police or community services can actually come into the schools and talk to the kids is a powerful one. I think that one of the biggest problems for school staff has always been that, no matter how good a teacher is, they just don't have the skills to deal with the types of problems that a lot of kids are facing these days. They aren't law enforcement or psychiatric professionals, yet they are expected to act in those roles sometimes. Frankly, the level of youth violence and crime has risen to the point in many schools where teachers spend just as much time policing hard-core kids as they do teaching the regular students who are actually there to learn. Enforcement just isn't the teachers' job.

PARTNERS FOR YOUTH

"There's actually a program called Partners for Youth in Edmonton that has placed counseling services, a psychiatric nurse, recreation coordinator, police officer, welfare worker and probation officer in a classroom within the schools. I'd like to see that trend continue and expand to schools across the country."

TACKLE VIOLENCE

At that point Robert raised his hand and asked, "So how are the schools and the police working together?"

"Well, Robert, my Tackle Violence course is one major way," I said. "I think it is a good example of how schools and police can work together to prevent youth violence. I am completely dependent on the partnership between the police and the schools in every community. I go and talk first to the school staff, the principals, the trustees and the teachers. Then I talk to the parents and the student body.

"I travel to high schools and elementary schools, speaking to thousands of students, making it very clear to them what youth violence is, showing them what happens as a result of youth violence and teaching them how to prevent it. We tried to make the video accessible to the kids by adding music and getting athletes and musicians to appear in it.

"My approach is getting a lot of good feedback, not just from educators and parents but from the kids themselves. After every talk I'm approached by a few students who offer me encouragement, thank me for coming to their school or have questions about their own situations.

"But my program is just one example of police-school liaisons. The Badge and the Book study done recently by the Solicitor General revealed that school-police liaisons are effective. Kids start seeing that 'the system works.' Once the students learn to trust the officers and feel comfortable telling them what they have seen and what they're worried about, then the officers can step in to address those concerns. The confidence of the kids then grows, because they see a positive action coming from their efforts. And more kids are likely to come forward if they encounter a problem. The students see that they are not going to face retaliation, and that speaking up is an effective way of dealing with a frightening situation.

"I've talked to officers who say they talk to more kids everyday about their private lives and personal problems than the school guidance counselor. It's all about gaining trust and becoming a genuine part of their lives. If they perceive you're just acting out of some obligation or you're not genuinely interested in them, their lives and their problems, then they lose confidence in you, and don't allow you to help them when they really need it.

"If you need stats on how effective and widespread these programs are, there is an excellent study done by the Brighter Futures Coalition which shows that about half of all Canadian school boards have some kind of joint program with their local police."

Robert said, "How do the teachers or the other school staff feel about that?"

I looked over at John and nodded for him to answer, "Well," John said, standing and adjusting his glasses. "For me there are some really big pluses to having a police officer around, aside from the ones Kevin has mentioned. First, I have found that in our district we are dealing more successfully with violent incidents than ever before. That's a fact. And I would put that down to, in part, our recent decision to allow the police to work in our schools. I mean, now our teachers and staff can judge each incident on the specifics of the situation and respond in any number of ways. They can apply school-based discipline, like suspension or expulsion, or they can apply criminal proceedings, like a caution or an arrest. And that's really the heart of the matter. Let's face it, our teachers were trained to teach. That's what they do best. But recently they've been forced into enforcement and policing roles in the classrooms and hallways against their will. That's just the way it is. Society is getting more and more violent, despite recent drops, crime has been on the rise for the past twenty years, and our schools are not immune to that trend. So imagine what a relief it is for your son's grade ten teacher to be able to call a police officer, someone that he sees on a regular basis and knows quite well, someone who is familiar with the kids in his class, and ask for advice about a specific student or a situation that seems to be developing. Even if that police officer never makes an arrest in one of our schools, the benefits to having him around are huge "– for teachers and students alike.

"If you need evidence that these programs work, I know that other principals in this district have reported that the number of intruders onto school property has declined since people realized that we would contact the police and they would respond immediately."

"Thanks, John," I said. "I should point out that kids also appreciate police officers being available to the schools. They feel safe and, don't forget, most kids under the age of 13 or 14 actually like cops." Laughter spread through the room. "As crazy as that sounds, younger children aren't yet at an age where they are challenging authority. They don't share the older kids' perceptions. They're just kids and, in my experience, they are fascinated by us, by and large. So try not to picture school-police liaisons as an armed camp; it's actually a lot more friendly than that."

WHAT IS STUDENT CRIME STOPPERS?

At the back of the room Lydia raised her hand and then said, "Kevin, I keep hearing about Student Crime Stoppers programs in other schools. Could you tell us what that's all about? Is it connected to the Crime Stoppers program that we see on TV?"

"Good question," I replied, smiling. "Actually, Student Crime Stoppers did grow out of the Crime Stoppers program and it does use the same principles. Both levels of this program rely on the public or the students in a particular school to phone a direct police hotline to leave tips about crimes that they are aware of. The key in both cases is that the callers are guaranteed anonymity. This means that everyone can feel safe if they ever need to report a crime and are worried about retaliation. As well, information leading to an arrest is rewarded."

"But does it really work?" asked Lydia. "I've heard kids saying they'd never rat on a friend or another student. Half of them seem too afraid to turn somebody else in to the police."

"The stats I've seen in the past few years show that it is working. According to the Safe Schools/Crime Stoppers protocol package there are over 650 Crime Stoppers programs operating world-wide and more than 80 of those are in Canada. Over 90% of all crimes that go to court based on Crime Stoppers leads result in a conviction. That's a great rate. And, in some schools, the crime rate has been reduced by up to 95%.

"To me the biggest advantage to this program is that it gives an outlet to the large percentage of the student body who don't commit crimes."

"But I'm not aware of a Crime Stoppers program at this school," said Lydia.

I nodded and said, "No, you're right. This school doesn't have a Crime Stoppers program at the moment. But they're not that hard to set up. That's where you, as parents, the primary care-givers in your neighbourhood can help. I'd suggest that you contact the Canadian Police Association or Crime Stoppers International and they will send you some material that leads you through the steps involved in setting up a program for this school. It's really very easy, but you should consult the organizations I named so that you can benefit from the good things other groups have done before you. I've found them very helpful in the past.

"My only caution is that you are careful not to rely too heavily on programs like Student Crime Stoppers. Some people find it sad, in a way, that a system exists that must pay people to do the right thing. It protects their anonymity as well, which reinforces the trend towards not getting involved. Basically, you can't ignore the fact that kids have to learn to get involved in situations and resolve them, like they do in peer mediation programs.

"I hope that gives you a good overview of both the reactive and preventative programs that schools and police departments have in place to help combat youth violence. And remember, together we form The Prevention Triangle, with our children in the centre for protection."

SOURCES

Ainsworth, Lynne. *Maintaining Safe Schools.* Toronto: Canadian Safe School Task Force, 1995.

Carey, Elaine. *"Canada's Crime Rate Falls For Fourth Year In A Row,"* The Toronto Star, July 31, 1996.

Carey, Elaine. *"Crime Rate's Down, Our Fears Are Up."* The Toronto Star, August 20, 1995.

Chisolm, Patricia, with David Thomas. *"Teenage Wasteland."* Maclean's, June 10, 1996.

Copple, P., Graham, J., Hornick, J.P., and Smith, R.B. *Community Resource Committee: A Community-Based Strategy For Dealing With Youth Crime And Violence In Calgary.* Calgary, Calgary Police Service, 1995.

Crime Stoppers International Inc. *Safe Schools/Crime Stoppers. (Protocol package)*

Durkan, Sean. *"Get-Tough Stance On Kids Nixed."* The Toronto Sun, July 9, 1996.

Gabor, Thomas. *School Violence And The Zero Tolerance Alternative: Some Principles And Policy Prescriptions.* Ottawa: Minister of Supply and Services, 1995.

Gerard, Warren. *"Psychiatrist Worries About Risk Facing Canada's Kids."* The Toronto Star, July 14, 1996.

Hess, Henry. *"U.S. Is Source Of Rising Flood Of Illegal Guns."* The Globe and Mail, May 13, 1995.

Howard, Ross. *"The Paradox Of Violence."* The Globe and Mail, March 23, 1996.

Makin, Kirk. *"Ontario Targets Young Offenders."* The Globe and Mail, June 3, 1996.

Mathews, Frederick. *Youth Gangs On Youth Gangs.* Toronto: Central Toronto Youth Services, 1993.

Mathews, Frederick. *The Badge & The Book.* Ottawa: Ministry of Supply and Service, 1995.

Psychology Today. *"Kindergarten Killers."* Psychology Today, March/April 1995.

Rincover, Dr. Arnold, *"Beat Gangs By Offering Alternatives."* The Ottawa Citizen, July 5, 1996.

Roberts, David. *"The Street Gangs Of Winnipeg."* The Globe and Mail, May 18, 1996.

Canadian Centre For Justice Statistics. *Canadian Crime Statistics.* Statistics Canada, 1996 (Catalogue No. 85-205).

Vincent, Isabel. *"Toronto's Gangs A Simmering Reality."* The Globe and Mail, August 5, 1995.

Vincent, Isabel. *"Girl-Gang Violence Alarms Experts."* The Globe and Mail, September 12, 1995.

Walker, Sandra Gail. *Weapons Use In Canadian Schools.* Ottawa: Ministry of Supply and Services, 1994.

Wright, Lisa. *"Can Boot Camp Help Young Offenders?"* The Toronto Star, August 6, 1996.

Are you interested in having a member
of Communities Against Youth Violence come
speak to your employees or members
of your organization?

ARE YOU INTERESTED IN ORDERING COPIES OF

THIS BOOK AT A SIGNIFICANT DISCOUNT

FOR YOUR EMPLOYEES OR MEMBERS OF YOUR ORGANIZATION?

Are you interested in receiving information on upcoming parenting conferences?

YOU CAN REACH US AT:

TELEPHONE:
IN TORONTO CALL **(416) 422-4806**
ELSEWHERE IN CANADA AND THE U.S. CALL
1-800-498-CAYV (2298)

FAX: (416) 422-1579

SEND E-MAIL TO cayv@interlog.com

MAILING:
COMMUNITIES AGAINST YOUTH VIOLENCE
621 MILVERTON BLVD.
TORONTO, ONTARIO, CANADA
M4C 1X8

VISIT OUR WEBSITE
www.interlog.com/~cayv